FAMOUS MEN OF GREECE
Teacher Guide

Leigh Lowe

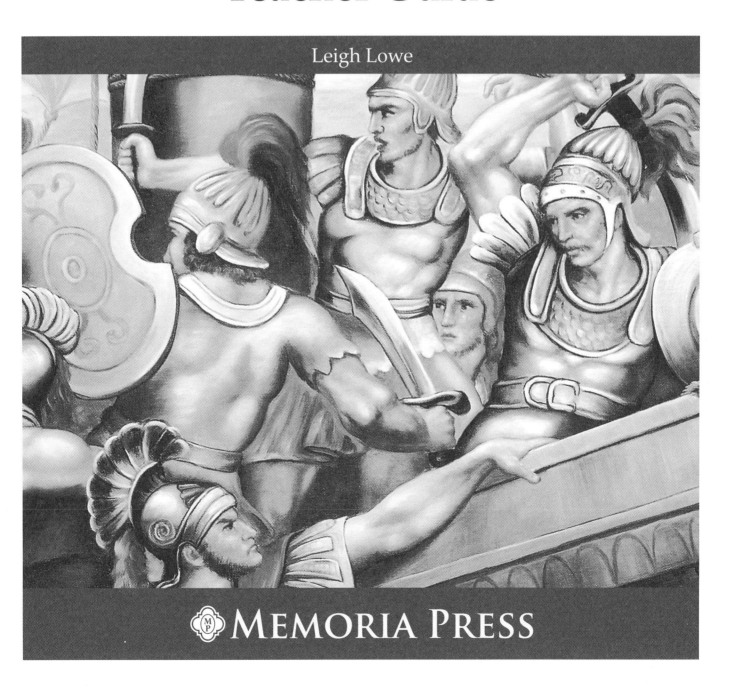

MEMORIA PRESS

MEMORIA PRESS

www.MemoriaPress.com

FAMOUS MEN OF GREECE
TEACHER GUIDE
Leigh Lowe

ISBN 978-1-5477-0200-8

Second Edition © 2019 Memoria Press | 0821

CONTENTS

HOW TO USE THIS GUIDE

FACTS TO KNOW

This section highlights the most important information in the *Famous Men of Greece* textbook. It is laid out in a format that is easy to read with clear and concise definitions for each noteworthy fact. This section should be the foundation of memory work and should be drilled throughout the year. Ideally, a student who has reviewed this material should be able to recite all of the information in each of the Facts to Know sections. Use the bold-faced words as prompts and require students to recite definitions. If you are interested in copybook work, this is the best section to have students neatly rewrite in a separate notebook.

VOCABULARY

We notice that students often skim over difficult vocabulary in subjects other than spelling, writing, English, or grammar. The *Famous Men of Greece* text is rich with interesting and advanced vocabulary. We have identified words that might be new or challenging to students so they can be defined or discussed either before reading or as the words come up in the stories. This section also includes specialized Greek history vocabulary words which deserve extra attention. We find that learning new vocabulary words in context rather than from dictionary definitions helps make the words more memorable and easier to understand. Try to locate the words in the text. Discuss the meaning and spelling of these words. Think of other places where challenging words have appeared, i.e., as a Latin derivative or in a piece of literature. It is generally better for students to learn new vocabulary from a teacher who can flesh out connotations. Use the words in this section for spelling and vocabulary tests. Students may also rewrite the words as a copybook exercise.

COMPREHENSION QUESTIONS

The comprehension questions in this book have been thoughtfully prepared to glean the most valuable information from the stories and direct students to identify the virtues and follies of the principals. It is best for students to write answers as complete sentences and practice proper punctuation and capitalization. The answers provided are often quite detailed. They are guides for the teacher and not necessarily what you should expect from your student. Your student's answers will depend on his or her age and scholastic level. If your student has large handwriting, use a separate notebook for comprehension questions.

ACTIVITIES

This section incorporates enrichment activities that help a student see the context of the stories in the book with timelines, family trees, maps, discussion questions, and research and writing prompts. The Activities section also offers drawing assignments and quotation memorization aids. The Teacher's Guide contains additional discussions and questions that the teacher may use and adapt to the age and scholastic level of the student. Drawing pages are provided after each Review Lesson.

APPENDIX

The Appendix section contains a timeline, worksheets, and maps.

LESSON 1: *The Gods of Greece, Sections I-II*

FACTS TO KNOW

1. **Cronos** – first king of the gods; swallowed his own children

2. **Rhea** – wife of Cronos

3. **Zeus (Jupiter)** – son of Cronos and Rhea; saved by Rhea; name means "brightness"; known by the Romans as Jupiter; became king of the gods by defeating Cronos

4. **Titans** – giants who aided Cronos in his battle against Zeus; hurled mountains

5. **Cyclops** – "round-eye"; giants who made thunder and lightning for Zeus

6. **Hera (Juno)** – sister of Zeus; queen of the gods; goddess of the clouds

7. **Poseidon (Neptune)** – brother of Zeus; god of the ocean

8. **Hades (Pluto)** – brother of Zeus; god of the underworld

9. **Demeter (Ceres)** – sister of Zeus; goddess of the grains, fruits, flowers

10. **Hestia (Vesta)** – sister of Zeus; goddess of fire and the hearth

11. **Styx** – river around the underworld; "hateful"

12. **Charon** – ferryman of the Styx

13. **Cerberus** – watchdog of the underworld

14. **Persephone (Proserpine)** – goddess of the underworld; daughter of Demeter

15. **nymphs** – maidens; helpers of Demeter

VOCABULARY

1. **constellation** _____ a group of stars _____

2. blood-red **coral** _____ rocklike skeletal remains of a small marine animal _____

3. shining **mother-of-pearl** _____ the pearly internal layer of certain mollusk shells _____

4. with his **trident** in his hand _____ a three-pronged fork or spear _____

5. **brazen** hoofs of the horses _____ resembling brass _____

6. world of Pluto was a **dreary** region. _____ dismal; bleak; dull _____

COMPREHENSION QUESTIONS

1. Why was Zeus at risk and how was he saved?

   Cronos' mother told him that one of his children would take his kingdom. So he
   swallowed each of his children as soon as they were born. His wife Rhea saved his
   son Zeus by tricking Cronos into swallowing a rock wrapped in baby clothes in Zeus'
   place. She then hid the child in a cave, which he filled with light.

2. Describe the battle between Cronos and Zeus.

When Zeus grew up, he went to war against Cronos. Cronos had the help of the mountain-throwing giants called Titans, and Zeus had the help of the Cyclops, who made the thunder and lightning that Zeus used as weapons. When the Titans hurled mountains, Zeus hurled back thunder and lightning.

3. What did Zeus do after his victory?

Zeus made Cronos restore to life the children he had swallowed. He divided Cronos' kingdom among them, so they became the gods and goddesses of the world. He made himself king of the gods and his sister Hera queen of the gods.

4. What is the Greek story of the seasons?

No goddess was willing to live with Hades, so he abducted Persephone and took her to the underworld with him. Zeus took pity on her and allowed her to return to the earth for a part of each year. When she comes to the earth, it is Spring and Summer, and the flowers bloom. When she leaves, it is Fall and Winter.

5. What is the story of the fruits, grains, and flowers?

In the Spring, Demeter causes the fruits, grains, and flowers to grow. She does this with the help of the tree nymphs who make the leaves green and the water nymphs who water the plants.

ACTIVITIES

1. Draw a family tree including Cronos, Rhea, Zeus, Hera, Poseidon, Hades, Demeter, Persephone, and Hestia. Start this on a large sheet of paper and keep it, as you will be adding to it.

2. Look at the maps in the back of this guide. Familiarize yourself with the shape of Greece, the Ægean Sea, and Asia Minor. Familiarize yourself with the main regions: Peloponnesus, Attica, Epirus, Thessaly, Macedonia, Thrace, Crete, the Ægean Sea, Asia Minor.

3. Make a list in two columns. Put the names of the Greek gods from this lesson in the left column. Put their corresponding Roman names in the right column. Leave plenty of room at the bottom of your list for additions. (See Appendix "Greek Gods and Their Roman Names")

LESSON 2: *The Gods of Greece, Sections III-IV*

FACTS TO KNOW

1. **Hermes (Mercury)** – son of Zeus; messenger of the gods
2. **Hephaestus (Vulcan)** – son of Zeus; god of fire; friend of metalworkers
3. **Ares (Mars)** – son of Zeus; god of war
4. **Apollo** – son of Zeus; twin of Artemis (Diana); god of the sun
5. **Artemis (Diana)** – daughter of Zeus; twin of Apollo; goddess of the moon
6. **Athena (Minerva)** – daughter of Zeus; goddess of wisdom
7. **Aphrodite (Venus)** – goddess of love; most beautiful of the goddesses
8. **Eros (Cupid)** – son of Aphrodite; god of love
9. **Iris** – brought rainbow; bore messages from heaven
10. **three Graces** – sisters; made mortals gracious and lovable
11. **three Furies** – sisters; punished and tormented the wicked
12. **three Fates** – sisters; higher than all the gods and goddesses
13. **Olympus** – mountain in Greece; home of the gods

VOCABULARY

1. a great **forge** under Mount Ætna _____ a blacksmith's furnace for heating metals _____
2. their hair was **twined** [twine] with serpents. ___ to twist together _____

COMPREHENSION QUESTIONS

1. How were Zeus and Hera like mortals?
   Hera had a temper. She and Zeus often had bad quarrels.

2. How was Athena born?
   Zeus had a headache he could not get rid of. He called for Hephaestus, who split
   open his head with an ax. From the head of Zeus came Athena, clothed in armor.

3. Identify the gods and goddesses:
   Zeus: ___ king of the gods _____
   Hera: ___ queen of the gods _____
   Poseidon: ___ god of the sea _____
   Demeter: ___ goddess of grains, fruits, and flowers _____

Hestia: __goddess of fire and the hearth__

Hades: __god of the underworld__

Persephone: __goddess of the underworld__

Hermes: __messenger of the gods__

Hephaestus: __god of fire and the forge__

Ares: __god of war__

Apollo: __god of the sun__

Artemis: __goddess of the moon__

Athena: __goddess of wisdom__

Aphrodite: __goddess of love__

Eros: __god of love__

4. Identify:

three Graces: __made mortals gracious and lovely__

three Furies: __tormented and punished the wicked__

three Fates: __spun, measured, and cut the thread of life; determined what was to be__

ACTIVITIES

1. Locate on Maps 1, 4: Mt. Olympus & Mt. Aetna

2. Continue your family history of the Greek gods to include Hermes, Hephaestus, Ares, Apollo, Artemis, Athena, Aphrodite, and Eros.

3. Continue your list of Greek and Roman names of the gods. (See Appendix "Greek Gods and Their Roman Names.")

LESSON 3: *Deucalion and the Flood*

FACTS TO KNOW

1. **Hebe** – goddess of youth

2. **Muses** – nine goddesses of poetry, arts, sciences

3. **Prometheus** – Titan, "forethought"; stole fire from the gods and gave it to man[*]

4. **Deucalion** – son of Prometheus; survived the flood

5. **Pyrrha** – wife of Deucalion; survived the flood

6. **Parnassus** – mountain where Deucalion's ark landed

7. **Hellenes; Hellas** – the Greeks; Greece

"Cast behind you the bones of your mother!" – **Parnassus oracle**

VOCABULARY

1. feast upon **ambrosia** _____ food of the gods, especially fragrant and flavorful

2. and drink **nectar** from goblets of gold. sweet liquid secreted by flowers

3. from **goblets** of gold._____ drinking vessels with a stem and base

4. and the **Muses** [Muse] sang. _____ source of artistic inspiration

5. a deep **cleft** in the rocks._____ deep crack

6. An **oracle** it is! _____ prophetic deity; shrine or priestess of same

COMPREHENSION QUESTIONS

1. What are the useful arts, and how did men learn them?

   Athena taught people how to harness horses and plow and how to spin and weave.

   Demeter taught how to sow wheat and barley, harvest, and bake bread. Hephaestus

   taught how to make things of iron and brass such as plows, spades, hoes, and, of

   course, weapons.

   _____

   _____

   _____

---

*Not covered in the textbook.

2. How did Deucalion discover the oracle, and what did the oracle tell him?

On leaving the ark, while descending Mt. Parnassus, Deucalion peered into a cleft in the ground. A wonderful voice spoke to him, saying, "Cast behind you the bones of your mother." Deucalion understood that this was an oracle, and he tried to understand the meaning of the message.

3. How did Deucalion and Pyrrha repopulate Greece?

Deucalion decided that the message referred to the earth as the mother and rocks as its bones. As they went down the mountain, Deucalion and Pyrrha cleared their path of stones, which they cast behind them. These turned into bands of young men and women. Deucalion and Pyrrha taught these men and women the useful arts. Together they repopulated the land, built houses, and so on.

ACTIVITIES

1. Locate on Map 2: Mt. Parnassus

For the teacher: In studying classical mythology, it is important to understand that the ancients did not think, as we do, that something is either natural fact or untrue. The classical myths are *allegories*. The ancients saw these stories as true—not as natural fact, but true in a different way. Use the following questions to teach this important idea.

- What is an *allegory*? Is an allegory true?
  An allegory is a story about real things told in terms of mythical persons and events. The meaning of an allegory is true, or intended to be true, although the persons and events may not be factual. An allegory is a way to tell a story about an idea that is too complex and multifaceted to be told in a factual way, especially in view of the limited information about the natural world available to the ancients. Our ancient ancestors saw no conflict between allegorical truth and factual truth.

- Is the story of Deucalion allegorical? What does it explain?
  It is allegorical. It explains the origin of the historical Greek people, why they are called "Hellenes," and why their country is called "Hellas."

- Were the ancients primitive believers of giants in the sky, or did they have their own sophisticated, but different, way of understanding the world?
  The ancient allegories of complex natural phenomena and abstract ideas are powerful and sophisticated. They are certainly not primitive, and they continue to generate fresh ideas. Many films and TV shows use ideas and story lines from the ancient allegories.

LESSON 4: *Cadmus and the Dragon's Teeth*

FACTS TO KNOW

1. **Agenor** – king of Phoenicia
2. **Europa** – Agenor's beautiful daughter
3. **Cadmus** – son of Agenor; consulted the Parnassus oracle
4. **Thebes** – city founded by Cadmus
5. **Amphion** – magical musician; built the walls of Thebes with a lyre
6. **Harmony** – daughter of Venus; given to Cadmus as a wife

"Building is better than killing." – **Cadmus**

VOCABULARY

1. a fine **frolic** to take a ride ___ a joyful play; sport
2. **capering** [**caper**] over the meadow. ___ to play and leap about in a frisky way
3. the **din** of the battle. ___ loud, discordant noise

COMPREHENSION QUESTIONS

1. What is the story of Europa and the bull, and how did it affect Cadmus?

   Europa took a ride on a white bull that appeared where she and her brothers were
   playing. The bull carried her out to sea, from which she never returned, but instead
   ended up on the shores of Europe, the continent that now bears her name. Agenor
   sent Cadmus with his brothers to search for Europa, and his adventures began on
   that journey.

2. What did the oracle tell Cadmus, and what did he do?

   The oracle told Cadmus to follow a cow and build a city where it would lie down.
   Spotting a cow nearby, Cadmus and his companions followed it until finally it lay down.

3. What did Cadmus and his companions find when they camped for the night?

   They found an enchanted spring guarded by a dragon.

4. Describe the dragon and what happened to it.

   The dragon had the claws of a lion, the wings of an eagle, and the jaws of a serpent. The dragon sprang from behind a rock and killed all but Cadmus. Cadmus killed the dragon by plunging his sword down the creature's throat and into its heart. He heard the words "sow the dragon's teeth," which he did.

5. How did the oracle's prophecy result in the founding of Thebes?

   An armed man sprang from each sown tooth. Another voice commanded Cadmus to throw a stone among the warriors. When he did this, the warriors fought each other until all but five were dead. Cadmus set these to building a city, fulfilling the oracle's instructions and prophecy.

6. What was Cadmus' misfortune and fate?

   Cadmus was condemned to eight years of punishment for killing the dragon. After this, Zeus gave him Harmony as a wife. One of her wedding presents was a necklace that brought bad luck to all who wore it. Grieving from the misfortunes it produced, she and Cadmus went into exile in the west of Greece. Finally Zeus turned them into serpents and led them to the land of the blessed.

ACTIVITIES

1. Locate on Map 2: Thebes
2. Draw the dragon by the enchanted spring.

For the teacher:

- Is the story of Cadmus allegorical? What does it explain? Yes, it is allegorical. It explains the founding of Thebes.

- What can we learn from the story of Cadmus about the most important factors in the founding of an ancient city? The story tells that an ancient city needed a good source of water, good soil for farming, and a good wall for its defense.

LESSON 5: *Perseus (Περσεύς)*

FACTS TO KNOW

1. **Argos** – birthplace of Perseus
2. **Danaë** – daughter of the king of Argos
3. **Perseus** – son of Danaë; turned into a constellation
4. **Dictys** – fisherman who rescued Danaë and Perseus
5. **Polydectes** – brother of Dictys; ruler of Seriphos; fell in love with Danaë
6. **Gorgons** – three horrible sisters with snakes for hair
7. **Medusa** – the only mortal of the three Gorgons
8. **Gray Sisters** – told Perseus where the land of the Hesperides was
9. **Hesperides** – beautiful nymphs with magic treasures
10. **Andromeda** – to be sacrificed to Poseidon; rescued by and married to Perseus; turned into a constellation
11. **Cepheus, Cassiopeia** – king and queen; parents of Andromeda; turned into constellations

"See! I have brought you that which you desired." – **Perseus**

"What had been fated came to pass." – **Greek saying**

VOCABULARY

1. While playing **quoits** one day _____ gamepieces; rings of iron to be pitched at a stake _____

COMPREHENSION QUESTIONS

1. How did Perseus end up on Seriphos, and what happened there?

   The king of Argos was told by an oracle that Perseus, the son of his daughter Danaë, would kill him. So he cast them both adrift on the sea in a chest. The chest landed on Seriphos, where Danaë and Perseus were rescued by the brother of the king. The king wanted to marry Danaë, but she refused. Later, when he was to marry another, he asked Perseus to bring him the head of the Gorgon Medusa as a gift.

2. Describe Perseus' journey to find Medusa, who helped him, and so on.

   Hermes offered his sword of light, Athena her shield, and both would guide Perseus to the Grey Sisters. Finding the Gray Sisters asleep, Perseus took the eye and tooth they shared, and by withholding them, he forced the sisters to reveal the location of the land of the Hesperides. The Hesperides loaned Perseus winged sandals of gold, a magic wallet for Medusa's head, and a cap of invisibility.

3. How was Perseus able to take Medusa's head, and why did it require special handling?

Perseus cut off Medusa's head without looking at it. The sight of a Gorgon's head turns one to stone. Using the cap of invisibility and the winged sandals, Perseus escaped the other Gorgons.

4. Who was Andromeda, and how did she end up marrying Perseus?

Andromeda had been chained at the shore by her parents as a sacrifice to Poseidon, who had been inflicting storms and a monster on the land after Andromeda's mother bragged that Andromeda was more beautiful than Poseidon's nymphs. Perseus cut her loose and killed the monster using the sword of light and the cap of invisibility. For his heroism and her sacrifice, the two were married in a joyful ceremony.

5. Why was Poseidon angry with King Cepheus' people?

Cassiopeia, Andromeda's mother, bragged that Andromeda was more beautiful than Poseidon's nymphs.

6. What happened back on Seriphos?

Perseus took Andromeda back to Seriphos to give Medusa's head to Polydectes. When he pulled the head from the magic wallet, Polydectes and his men were turned to stone. Perseus gave the head as an offering to Athena, returned the sword, sandals, wallet, and cap, and returned to Argos.

7. How was the fate of the king of Argos fulfilled?

Perseus became good friends with the king of Argos but accidentally killed him in a game of quoits. Perseus, now king of Argos but overwhelmed with sorrow, exchanged his kingdom for the kingdom of Tiryns. After their deaths, he and Andromeda became stars in the sky.

ACTIVITIES

1. Locate on Maps 1, 2: Argos, Seriphos, Tiryns
2. Draw a picture of a Gorgon.

For the teacher:

- What conflicting qualities are apparent in the appearance of Medusa? She is both very beautiful and extremely terrifying. We see here an illustration of all humanity—beautiful and horrid at the same time.

- The meaning of allegory is often very complex. What are two possible meanings of being "turned to stone"? Frozen in fear, or killed. Explore other aspects of the symbolism, such as "like a statue," etc. (spiritually dead, insensitive, emotionally dead)

REVIEW LESSON 1: *Lessons 1-5*

GREEK GODS AND GODDESSES

Cronos	1.	first king of the gods
Rhea	2.	wife of Cronos
Zeus	3.	his son; king of the Olympian gods
Hera	4.	queen of the Olympian gods
Poseidon	5.	god of the ocean
Hades	6.	god of the underworld
Persephone	7.	goddess of the underworld
Demeter	8.	goddess of grains, fruits, flowers, harvest
Hermes	9.	messenger of the gods
Hephaestus	10.	god of fire
Hestia	11.	goddess of fire and the hearth
Ares	12.	god of war
Apollo	13.	god of the sun
Artemis	14.	goddess of the moon and of the hunt
Athena	15.	goddess of wisdom
Aphrodite	16.	goddess of love
Eros	17.	god of love
Hebe	18.	goddess of youth
Muses	19.	goddesses of poetry, arts, sciences

OTHER PEOPLE AND PLACES OF GREEK MYTHOLOGY

Titans	1.	giants who aided the first king of the gods
Cyclopes	2.	giants who aided the first king of the gods' son
Styx	3.	river around the underworld
Charon	4.	ferryman of the underworld
Cerberus	5.	watchdog of the underworld
nymphs	6.	helpers of the goddess of grains, fruits, flowers
Iris	7.	brought rainbow; bore messages from heaven
three Graces	8.	made mortals gracious and lovable

three Furies	**9.**	punished and tormented the wicked
three Fates	**10.**	spun, controlled, and cut the thread of life
Mt. Olympus	**11.**	home of the gods

HEROES, DEMIGODS, AND SEMIHISTORICAL FIGURES

Prometheus	**1.**	stole fire from the gods and gave it to man
Deucalion	**2.**	man who survived the flood
Pyrrha	**3.**	wife who survived the flood
Cadmus	**4.**	founder of Thebes
Harmony	**5.**	wife of the founder of Thebes
Gorgon	**6.**	monster whose gaze turned men to stone
Perseus	**7.**	cut off the monster's head
Andromeda	**8.**	wife of Perseus
Medusa	**9.**	only mortal among the three Gorgons
Hesperides	**10.**	nymphs with magic treasures

WHO SAID THAT?

1. "Cast behind you the bones of your mother!" _____ Parnassus oracle

2. "Building is better than killing." _____ Cadmus

3. "See! I have brought you that which you desired." _____ Perseus

4. "What had been fated came to pass." _____ Greek saying

COMPREHENSION QUESTIONS TO REVIEW

1. How did Zeus become king of the gods?

   When Zeus grew up, he went to war against Cronos. Zeus was victorious and made
   Cronos restore to life the children he had swallowed. He divided Cronos' kingdom
   among them, so they became the gods and goddesses of the world. He made himself
   king of the gods and his sister Hera queen of the gods.

2. What is the Greek story of the seasons, the fruits, grains, and flowers?

Hades abducted Persephone and took her to the underworld. Zeus took pity on her and allowed her to return to the earth for a part of each year. When she comes to the earth, it is Spring and Summer. When she leaves, it is Fall and Winter. In the Spring, Demeter causes the fruits, grains, and flowers to grow, with the help of the tree nymphs who make the leaves green, and the water nymphs who water the plants.

3. How was Greece repopulated after the flood?

Deucalion decided that the oracle's message referred to the earth as the mother and rocks as its bones. As they went down the mountain, Deucalion and Pyrrha cleared their path of stones, which they cast behind them. These turned into bands of young men and women. Deucalion and Pyrrha taught these men and women the useful arts. Together they repopulated the land.

4. Recount the story of the founding of Thebes.

Armed men sprang from the dragon's teeth sown by Cadmus. A voice commanded Cadmus to throw a stone among the warriors. When he did this, the warriors fought each other until all but five were dead. Cadmus set these to building a city, fulfilling the oracle's instructions and prophecy.

5. How was Perseus' fate fulfilled?

Perseus became good friends with the king of Argos, but accidentally killed him in a game of quoits. Perseus, now king of Argos but overwhelmed with sorrow, exchanged his kingdom for the kingdom of Tiryns. After their deaths, he and Andromeda became stars in the sky.

VOCABULARY

twine	forge	oracle	constellation	brazen	quoit
trident	ambrosia	nectar	caper	mother-of-pearl	cleft
din	coral	goblet	dreary	muse	frolic

muse	**1.** source of artistic inspiration
brazen	**2.** resembling brass
quoit	**3.** ring of iron to be pitched at a stake
goblet	**4.** a drinking vessel with stem and base
caper	**5.** to leap about in a frisky way
twine	**6.** to twist together
coral	**7.** skeletal remains of small marine animal
dreary	**8.** bleak; dull
oracle	**9.** prophetic deity
din	**10.** loud, discordant noise
mother-of-pearl	**11.** the internal layer of mollusk shell
cleft	**12.** deep crack
forge	**13.** blacksmith's furnace
frolic	**14.** to play joyfully
nectar	**15.** the sweet liquid secreted by flowers
constellation	**16.** a group of stars
ambrosia	**17.** food of the gods
trident	**18.** a three-pronged spear

GEOGRAPHY REVIEW: *Study the location of the following places.*

Cities
- Thebes
- Argos

Bodies of Water, Mountains
- Mt. Olympus
- Mt. Parnassus

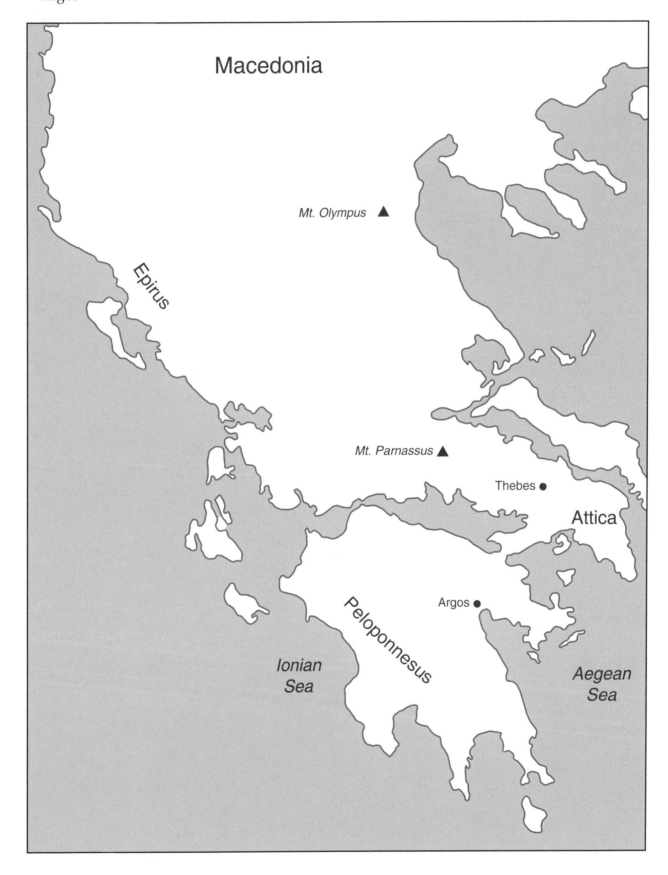

GEOGRAPHY REVIEW: *Use the following places to complete the maps.*

Cities
- Thebes
- Argos

Bodies of Water, Mountains
- Mt. Olympus
- Mt. Parnassus

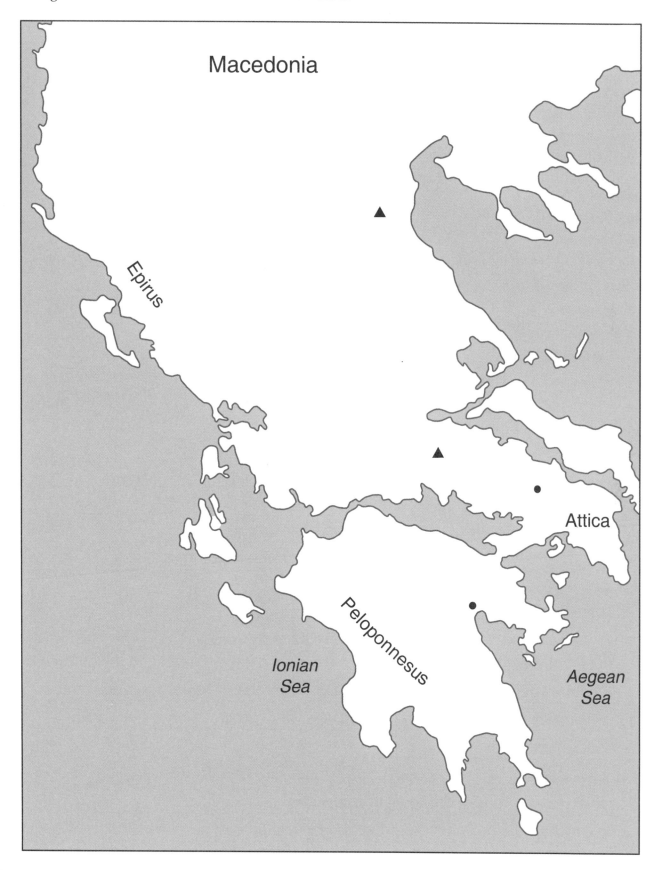

LESSON 6: *Hercules (Ἡρακλῆς) and His Labors*

FACTS TO KNOW

1. **Herakles (Hercules)** – greatest of the Greek heroes; mortal son of Zeus

2. **Eurystheus** – king of Mycenæ; cousin of Hercules

3. **12 labors of Hercules** –
   - kill the Nemean lion
   - kill the hydra of Lerna
   - bring the stag with golden horns sacred to Artemis
   - kill the boar of Mt. Erymanthus
   - clean the Augean stables
   - kill the birds of Lake Stymphalus
   - bring the bull of Crete
   - tame the horses of Diomedes
   - get the girdle of queen Hippolyte of the Amazons
   - bring the oxen of Geryon
   - get golden apples of the Hesperides
   - bring Cerberus, watchdog of the underworld

4. **Atlas** – held up the sky; father of the Hesperides

5. **Admetus; Alcestis** – king and queen of Thessaly

6. **Omphale** – queen of Lydia

7. **Deianira** – wife of Hercules

8. **Nessus** – centaur; tried to abduct Deianira

"I will get you some of the apples if you will hold up the sky for me." – **Atlas**

VOCABULARY

1. by burning each neck with a **firebrand** ___a piece of burning wood___

2. the **stag** with golden horns___adult male deer___

3. a way to tame the savage **steeds**. ___spirited horses___

4. the **girdle** of the queen of the Amazons. ___a belt or sash___

5. Nessus, the **centaur**___mythological creature: half-man, half-horse___

COMPREHENSION QUESTIONS

1. Describe how Hercules got off to a rough start and was obliged to perform twelve labors.

   Hera, queen of the gods, hated Hercules and sent two large serpents to devour him. He killed the serpents. In early manhood, he was forced by the gods to become the slave of his cousin Eurystheus, king of Mycenæ, who required of him twelve labors, actually designed to kill him.

2. Briefly describe each of the labors and how Hercules accomplished it.

   1. kill the Nemean lion; H. choked it in a cave and skinned it

   2. kill the hydra of Lerna; a friend burned the necks to prevent new heads from growing

3. bring the stag sacred to Artemis; H. chased it for a year

4. kill the boar of Mt. Erymanthus; H. captured it in a net

5. clean the Augean stables; H. diverted two rivers so that they ran through the filthy stables

6. kill the birds of L. Stymphalus; H. killed them with poisoned arrows

7. bring bull of Crete; H. conquered the bull, rode it across the sea, then carried it on his shoulder

8. tame the horses of Diomedes; H. killed Diomedes and fed his flesh to the horses

9. get the girdle of Hippolyte; H. killed Hippolyte in a battle engineered by Hera's trickery

10. bring the oxen of Geryon; with the help of Apollo's golden bowl

11. get golden apples of the Hesperides; H. held up the sky while Atlas got the apples

12. bring Cerberus from underworld; on the advice of Hades, H. overcame Cerberus without weapons

3. Describe Hercules' spell of insanity.

While insane, Hercules killed a beloved friend. For this the gods made him ill. Apollo refused to cure him so he tried to carry off the tripod of the priestess of Delphi. For this he was deprived of his strength and given to Omphale as a slave, who dressed him as a woman and made him do woman's work.

4. Describe the deed Hercules performed for his friend Admetus.

Admetus' wife, Alcestis, gave her life so Admetus could live. Hercules went to Hades, seized Alcestis, and returned her to her grieving husband.

5. Describe the death of Hercules and the part his wife played in it.

Hercules killed the centaur Nessus that was trying to abduct Deianira. The centaur told Deianira to save some of its blood, which she did. Years later, in a fit of jealousy, she put this blood on Hercules' robe, thinking it had the power to make Hercules love her more. It burned his skin and killed him. His body was cremated and his spirit rose to the heavens, where he was welcomed as one of the gods.

ACTIVITIES

1. Locate on Maps 1-3:
   - Mycenae
   - forest of Nemea
   - marsh of Lerna
   - Arcadia
   - Mt. Erymanthus
   - Lake Stymphalus
   - Crete
   - Thrace
   - Black Sea
   - Thessaly
   - Delphi
   - Lydia

For the teacher: Have each student act out one of the labors of Hercules, or tell it as a story, complete with sound effects and dramatic elements.

LESSON 7: *Jason (Ἰάσων) and the Golden Fleece*

FACTS TO KNOW

1. **Pelias** – king of Iolcus; usurped throne from his older brother Æson

2. **Jason** – son of Æson

3. **Chiron** – centaur; most famous teacher in Greece; raised Jason

4. **Phrixus** – nailed golden fleece on a tree sacred to Ares

5. **Helle** – sister of Phrixus; drowned in the strait (Hellespont) that bears her name

6. **Æetes** – king of Colchis

7. **Argo** – Jason's ship

8. **Argonauts** – sailors on Jason's expedition

9. **Orpheus** – greatest musician of mythical Greece

10. **Castor and Pollux** – twins; sailed with Jason; turned into a constellation

11. **Lynceus** – "lynx-eyed"; sailed with Jason

12. **Medea** – daughter of Æetes; fell in love with Jason and helped him

13. **Sirens** – beautiful maidens; lured sailors to crash on the rocks

"Beware of the man who wears but one sandal." – **oracle of Apollo**

VOCABULARY

1. the golden **fleece** _____ sheep's coat of wool

2. the **prow** of the vessel. _____ the front part of a ship

3. play his **lyre** and sing. _____ a handheld harp-like instrument, used to accompany song or poetry

4. **yoke** my pair of … bulls _____ bar for joining two draft animals

5. the field was … **harrowed** [harrow]. _____ to break up earth using a plow-like tool with teeth

COMPREHENSION QUESTIONS

1. Why did Pelias fear Jason would try to kill him and take his throne?

   Pelias usurped Aeson's throne when Jason, Aeson's son, was a boy. After the 20 years that Jason was missing, Pelias consulted the oracle of Apollo, who warned him of a man with one sandal. When Jason entered Iolcus as an adult, he was only wearing one sandal.

2. Describe Jason's encounter with Hera on his journey to Iolcus.

   Hera, disguised as an old woman, was trying to cross a swollen stream and Jason carried her across. She was testing the kindness of men and never forgot Jason's courtesy to her.

3. Why did Jason make a voyage to retrieve the golden fleece?

   When Jason arrived to confront Pelias, Pelias agreed to yield the crown after Jason returned with the golden fleece, a nearly impossible task.

4. What was the golden fleece and how was it protected?

    A Grecian king was about to sacrifice his son Phrixus on orders of Zeus when a ram with a fleece of gold came from the sky and rescued the son. They went to Colchis, where Phrixus sacrificed the ram to Zeus and nailed it on a tree sacred to Ares, where it was guarded by a dragon.

5. Name five of the Argonauts and their special talents.

    Orpheus with his magical lyre; Hercules with his exceptional strength; Castor and Pollux who performed such wonders that after their deaths they were made into a constellation; Lynceus the lynx-eyed who could see a day's trip ahead.

6. How did Æetes make the task difficult for Jason, and why?

    The fleece was the great prize of Æetes' kingdom and he did not want to lose it. He gave Jason a task designed to get him killed—to plow the field near the fleece with fire-breathing bulls, to sow the field with some of the teeth of the dragon Cadmus had killed, and, finally, to fight the dragon that guards the fleece.

7. How did Jason get the fleece? Who was Medea, and what part did she play?

    Medea, Æetes' daughter, fell in love with Jason and helped him. She gave him ointment as protection against the bulls. She told him to throw a rock into the warriors grown from the dragon's teeth, who proceeded to kill each other. She fed the dragon protecting the fleece a sleeping potion. Thus, Jason was able to grab the fleece.

8. Describe Jason's return voyage and his ultimate fate.

    The Argo had to sail past the island of the Sirens. They did so with the help of Orpheus who played even more sweetly than the Sirens sang, giving Jason and his crew sufficient distraction to get past the Sirens. At Iolcus, Jason hung the fleece in a temple. But while he had been gone, Pelias had murdered Æson, Jason's father. Medea tried to avenge this by hatching a plot in which Pelias was killed by his own daughters, but she and Jason were driven out from Iolcus by Pelias' son.

ACTIVITIES

1. Locate on Map 6:
    - Iolcus
    - Colchis
    - Dodona
    - Hellespont (Dardanelles)
    - Euxine (Black Sea)

For the teacher: Have your students research more details about Jason's route and what he did along the way to Colchis. There are several good mythology sites online. Online, search: Greek mythology, Jason, Argonauts.

LESSON 8: *Theseus (Θησεύς)*

FACTS TO KNOW

1. **Cecrops** – wise Greek king; founder of Athens
2. **Theseus** – noted king of Athens; son of king Ægeus
3. **Æthra** – mother of Theseus
4. **Minos** – king of Crete; keeper of the Minotaur
5. **Minotaur** – monster of the Labyrinth
6. **Labyrinth** – winding maze where the Minotaur was kept
7. **Ariadne** – daughter of Minos; took pity on Theseus and helped him

"If you are a man, lift that stone." – **Æthra**

VOCABULARY

1. The **Labyrinth** was full of winding paths an intricate maze of interconnecting passages

COMPREHENSION QUESTIONS

1. How did Athens get its name?

   Athena and Poseidon quarreled over which would be the chief god of Cecrops' new city.
   Poseidon's argument was that it would be a great sea power, and Athena's was that it
   would be a great center of learning. In a contest set by Zeus, Poseidon produced a war
   horse and Athena produced an olive tree. Zeus decided that olive trees would benefit the
   city more than war horses, so Athena became the city's goddess and namesake.

2. Describe Theseus' adventures on his journey to Athens.

   First, a robber attacked Theseus with a club; Theseus killed the robber and kept the
   club. Then, he encountered a man who set traps with pine trees; Theseus put the
   man into his own trap. Finally, he encountered a man who stretched or cut men to fit a
   particular bed; Theseus cut the man to fit his own bed.

3. How did Theseus become heir to the throne of Athens?

Ægeus had placed sandals and a sword under a heavy stone, with instructions to Theseus' mother that when he could lift the stone, he should seek his father out in Athens. This took place, and when Theseus arrived in Athens with the sword, Ægeus declared him his heir.

4. Why did Theseus travel to Crete with thirteen other young Athenians?

Each year, seven young men and seven maidens had to be sent by Athens to Crete to be sacrificed to the Minotaur. Theseus went as one of the fourteen in order to defeat the Minotaur and end this annual sorrow for Athens.

5. How did Ariadne help Theseus with the Minotaur?

At the mouth of the Labyrinth, Ariadne handed Theseus a ball of thread, the end of which she would hold. By unraveling the ball, he would have a guide to find his way out.

6. How did Theseus become king of Athens?

In love with Ariadne but having to leave her behind on Naxos, Theseus was distracted. He forgot to raise a white sail that Ægeus would have recognized as a sign that he had survived the Minotaur, leaving a black one up instead, the sign of failure. Seeing this, Ægeus fell from a cliff and drowned in the sea that ever since bore his name. On the death of Ægeus, Theseus became king.

ACTIVITIES

1. Locate on Map 1:
   - Athens
   - Crete
   - Naxos
   - Aegean Sea

2. Design your own labyrinth. Experiment with the design of mazes. Place the Minotaur in the center.

3. Draw or paint the Minotaur, whose bottom half was a man and whose top half was a bull. If you are more skilled with words than with images, write a word-picture of the Minotaur. Online you will find ancient images of the Minotaur, painted on walls and vases.

LESSON 9: *Agamemnon (Ἀγαμέμνων) King of Men*

FACTS TO KNOW

1. **Agamemnon** – king of Mycenae during the Trojan War
2. **Peleus** – king of Thessaly
3. **Thetis** – wife of Peleus
4. **Paris** – shepherd appointed by Zeus to judge the dispute over which of three goddesses was most beautiful
5. **Priam** – father of Paris; king of Troy
6. **Menelaus** – king of Sparta; brother of Agamemnon
7. **Helen** – wife of Menelaus; her abduction set off the Trojan War
8. **Calchas** – Agamemnon's soothsayer
9. **Iphigenia** – Agamemnon's daughter; Artemis demanded her as a sacrifice but then saved her

"If my death will help the Greeks, I am ready to die." – **Iphigenia**

VOCABULARY

1. he was greatly **perplexed**. _____ confused; bewildered _____
2. he consulted a wonderful **soothsayer** _one who predicts events_ _____

COMPREHENSION QUESTIONS

1. How did a golden apple set the stage for the Trojan War?

   At the wedding of Peleus and Thetis, the uninvited goddess of discord tossed a golden
   apple with the inscription that it was to be given to the most beautiful of the goddesses.
   A quarrel erupted, and Zeus ordered that Paris, son of Priam, be sought out to decide.

2. Who was Paris, and how did he thicken the plot?

   Because his mother had dreamed that he would burn Troy down, Priam left his son
   Paris on Mt. Ida to die. Paris was rescued and raised by a shepherd. The goddesses
   came to him and each promised him a reward for deciding in her favor. He chose
   Aphrodite, who had promised him the most beautiful woman in the world as a wife.

3. How did Helen become a pretext for the war?

Helen, wife of King Menelaus of Sparta, was known as the most beautiful woman in the world. Paris went to Sparta and stole her away. Menelaus began preparing for war to regain his wife and punish Paris. He had the willing assistance of more than 30 other kings, all rejected suitors of Helen.

4. How did it happen that Artemis required the sacrifice of Iphigenia?

Agamemnon, brother of Menelaus, was also preparing for war. When he was almost ready, a terrible storm came up, which he believed to be the anger of one of the gods. A soothsayer told him that Artemis was angry with him for killing a deer on a hunt and bragging that he was a better hunter than Artemis herself. The soothsayer told Agamemnon he must sacrifice his daughter Iphigenia to Artemis.

5. What was the outcome?

Iphigenia was willing to submit to sacrifice if it would help the Greeks. Artemis took pity and saved her at the last moment and made her a priestess. A white fawn appeared on the altar in her place. Fair winds arose and the Greek fleet sailed for Troy.

ACTIVITIES

1. Locate on Maps 1-3:
- Mycenae
- Thessaly
- Mt. Pelion
- Mt. Ida
- Troy
- Sparta
- Aulis

2. Begin filling in the timeline of ancient Greece in the back of this guide, starting with the Trojan War.

For the teacher:

Although Troy is a real place that was devastated at least once in its history, it is not certain that the Trojan War as such actually took place. Begin learning some things about the historicity (historical authenticity) of the Trojan War—that is, which elements are likely to have happened and which elements are more likely mythical. Consider also that the real Trojan War may have been a series of wars. Online, search: Troy, Trojan War.

LESSON 10: *Achilles (Ἀχιλλεύς), Bravest of the Greeks*

FACTS TO KNOW

1. **Achilles** – bravest of the Greek warriors in the Trojan War; son of Peleus and Thetis
2. **Styx** – river around the underworld; rendered a human invulnerable
3. **Odysseus** – Greek chief; went to find Achilles
4. **Chryses** – father of Agamemnon's slave girl; priest of Apollo
5. **Priam** – king of Troy
6. **Hector** – son of Priam
7. **Patroclus** – fought in Achilles' armor; killed by Hector
8. **Thetis** – mother of Achilles; sea-nymph
9. **Palladium** – temple of Athena at Troy; protected Troy
10. **Pallas** – another name for Athena
11. **Andromache** – wife of Hector; given to the son of Achilles as captive

VOCABULARY

1. goddess of **discord** had thrown _____strife; dissension_____
2. a terrible **pestilence** into the camp ___disease; sickness_____

COMPREHENSION QUESTIONS

1. How was Achilles made almost invulnerable, and what was his one weakness?

   Achilles' mother, Thetis, could never die. To make her son immortal, she took him to the river Styx, which renders mortals dipped in it invulnerable. She immersed all of his body but the heel, by which she held him. His heel was Achilles' only vulnerable spot.

2. Why did his mother hide him away on an island, how was he found, and what followed?

   Thetis feared that Achilles would be killed in a war with Troy. But the soothsayer Calchas had foretold that the Greeks could not win without Achilles. Odysseus found Achilles by posing as a peddler and going to Scyros, the island of Achilles' refuge. When a war trumpet rang, all the girls ran away except one, who drew a sword. Odysseus knew he had found Achilles.

3. What made Achilles withdraw from fighting in the tenth year of the war?

Apollo was punishing the Greeks because Agamemnon had taken the daughter of
Apollo's priest captive. When forced to give her up, Agamemnon then took Achilles'
maiden captive. Achilles took to his tent for days, pouring his heart out to his mother,
and would not fight.

4. How did Hector get hold of the armor of Achilles?

Patroclus, Achilles' close friend, had been fighting in Achilles' armor. Apollo, fighting on
the side of the Trojans, shot Patroclus with an arrow from his silver bow. Hector killed
Patroclus and took the armor of Achilles.

5. How did Achilles get new armor, and how did he kill Hector? How did Achilles die?

Thetis went to the blacksmith Hephaestus and acquired new armor for Achilles. In this
he terrorized the Trojans and killed Hector, whose body he dragged three times around
the tomb of Patroclus. Paris avenged the death of Hector by wounding Achilles in his
vulnerable heel, from which he died.

6. How did the war end?

Odysseus stole the image of Athena from its temple inside of Troy, leaving the city
without its protector. He then had the Greeks build a huge horse, with which they were
able to infiltrate Troy after convincing its inhabitants that the horse would replace the
statue as protector. The Greeks sacked and burned the city.

ACTIVITIES

1. Locate on Map 1:
   - Scyros
   - Troy

For the teacher:

- Have your students continue their research into the historicity (historical authenticity) of the Trojan War.

- What ancient Greek poet and singer composed the story of the Trojan War as it has come down to us? What was the form of this composition? What is it called? Why were poets of this time also known as "singers"?
  Homer (whose historical authenticity is also open to question) composed the *Iliad* as an oral epic. Poets of his time were called "singers" because they chanted their stories in a rhythmic, musical style.

REVIEW LESSON 2: *Lessons 6-10*

MYTHOLOGY

Hercules _____   1. mortal son of Zeus who became a god

Deianira _____   2. wife of Hercules

Atlas _____   3. held up the sky

Omphale _____   4. queen of Lydia

Jason _____   5. went after the golden fleece

Argo _____   6. Jason's ship

Castor and Pollux _____   7. twins who sailed with Jason

Medea _____   8. fell in love with Jason and helped him

Cecrops _____   9. founder of Athens

Minotaur _____   10. monster of the Labyrinth

Theseus _____   11. hero who killed the monster

Minos _____   12. king of Crete and keeper of the monster

Ariadne _____   13. this king's daughter who took pity on the hero

Agamemnon _____   14. leader of the Greeks in the Trojan War

Iphigenia _____   15. daughter of Agamemnon

Paris _____   16. judged which goddess was most beautiful

Menelaus _____   17. king of Sparta in the Trojan War

Helen _____   18. her abduction was the pretext for the Trojan War

Achilles _____   19. the Greek champion in the Trojan War

Priam _____   20. king of Troy in the Trojan War

Hector _____   21. the Trojan champion and prince

Andromache _____   22. wife of Hector

Pallas _____   23. another name for Athena

Chiron _____   24. centaur who raised Jason

Orpheus _____   25. greatest musician of mythical Greece

Sirens _____   26. beautiful maidens who lured sailors to crash on rocks

Thetis _____   27. mother of Achilles

Calchas _____   28. Agamemnon's soothsayer

Odysseus	**29.** Greek chief who went to find Achilles
Chryses	**30.** priest of Apollo; father of Agamemnon's captive maiden
Patroclus	**31.** friend of Achilles who wore his armor

WHO SAID THAT?

1. "I will get you some of the apples if you will hold up the sky for me." _Atlas_

2. "Beware of the man who wears but one sandal." _oracle of Apollo_

3. "If you are a man, lift that stone." _Æthra_

4. "If my death will help the Greeks, I am ready to die." _Iphigenia_

COMPREHENSION QUESTIONS TO REVIEW

1. Describe two of Hercules' labors and how he accomplished them.

See Lesson 6, Comprehension Question #2.

2. How was Jason able to take the golden fleece?

Medea, Æetes' daughter, fell in love with Jason and helped him. She gave him ointment as protection against the bulls. She told him to throw a rock into the warriors grown from the dragon's teeth, who proceeded to kill each other. She fed the dragon protecting the fleece a sleeping potion. Thus Jason was able to grab the fleece.

3. How did Athens get its name?

Athena and Poseidon quarreled over which one would be the chief god of Cecrops' new city. Poseidon's argument was that it would be a great sea power, and Athena's was that it would be a great center of learning. In a contest set by Zeus, Poseidon produced a war horse and Athena produced an olive tree. Zeus decided that olive trees would benefit the city more than war horses, so Athena became the city's goddess and namesake.

4. How did the Trojan War start?

   Helen, wife of King Menelaus of Sparta, was known as the most beautiful woman in the world. Paris went to Sparta and stole her away. Menelaus began preparing for war to regain his wife and punish Paris. He had the willing assistance of more than 30 other kings, all rejected suitors of Helen.

5. What is the story behind the phrase "Achilles' heel"?

   Achilles' mother, Thetis, could never die. To make her son immortal, she took him to the river Styx, which renders mortals dipped in it invulnerable. She immersed all of his body but the heel, by which she held him. Achilles' heel was his only vulnerable spot.

VOCABULARY

soothsayer	lyre	steed	centaur	prow	harrow	fleece	stag
girdle	labyrinth	perplexed	discord	firebrand	pestilence	yoke	

prow	1.	the front part of a ship
stag	2.	adult male deer
labyrinth	3.	intricate maze
yoke	4.	bar for joining two draft animals
steed	5.	spirited horse
fleece	6.	sheep's coat of wool
soothsayer	7.	one who predicts events
girdle	8.	a belt or sash
firebrand	9.	a piece of burning wood
lyre	10.	a handheld harp-like instrument
perplexed	11.	confused; bewildered
centaur	12.	mythological creature: half-man, half-horse
harrow	13.	to break up the earth for farming
pestilence	14.	disease; sickness
discord	15.	strife; dissension

GEOGRAPHY REVIEW: *Study the location of the following places.*

Countries, Islands
- Crete

Cities
- Delphi
- Sparta
- Athens
- Troy

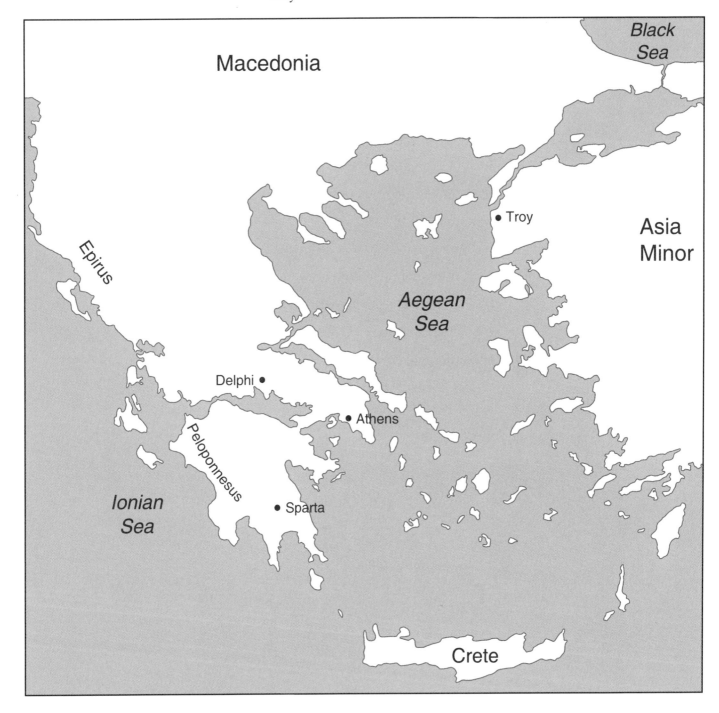

GEOGRAPHY REVIEW: *Use the following places to complete the maps.*

Countries, Islands
- Crete

Cities
- Delphi
- Sparta
- Athens
- Troy

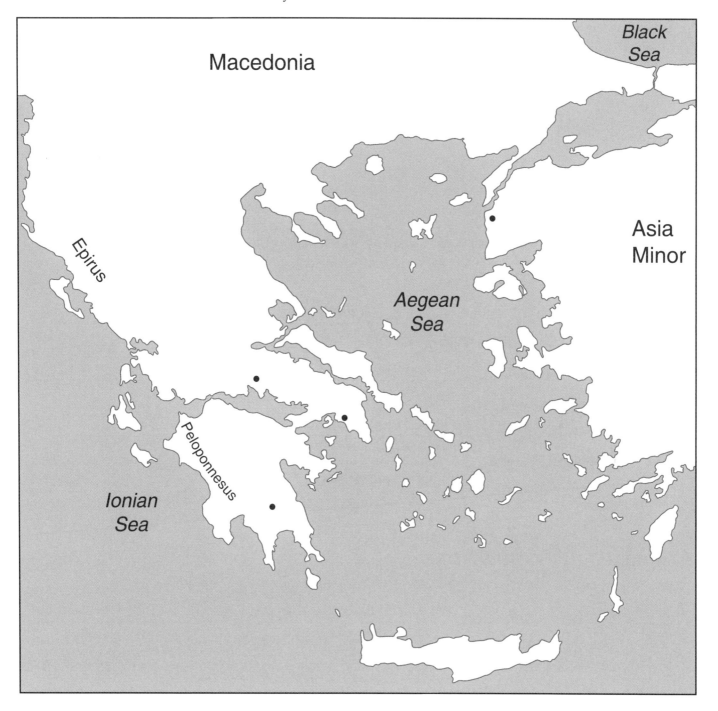

LESSON 11: *The Adventures of Odysseus (Ὀδυσσεύς)*

FACTS TO KNOW

1. **Odysseus** – king of Ithaca; reluctant hero of the Trojan War
2. **Telemachus** – son of Odysseus
3. **Cyclops (pl. Cyclopes)** – race of one-eyed giants
4. **Æolus** – god of the winds
5. **Eurylochus** – Odysseus' captain
6. **Circe** – sorceress; turned men into animals
7. **Scylla and Charybdis** – monster of the Strait of Messina; deadly whirlpool
8. **Calypso** – sea nymph; cared for Odysseus for seven years
9. **Nausicaa** – island princess; found Odysseus on the shore
10. **Penelope** – wife of Odysseus

"I care nothing for gods! But as for men, let me show you how much I like them!" – **Cyclops**

"Loose me! Loose me! I must go nearer that music!" – **Odysseus**

VOCABULARY

1. land of the **lotus**-eaters. ___fruit of a small tree (Greek mythology)___ (*not the Asian edible rhizome of the same name)
2. the mouth of a **cavern** ___large cave___
3. The pieces of beef **lowed [low]** ___to moo (characteristic cow sound)___
4. a dreadful **squall** blew up. ___a sudden, brief, violent windstorm___
5. a forest of **stately** pine trees. ___majestic; dignified; lofty___
6. a **shroud** for her father-in-law ___a burial cloth___
7. **haughtily** tried to string ___with scornful pride___
8. **odyssey** ___long adventurous voyage___

COMPREHENSION QUESTIONS

1. Who was Odysseus, how did he end up at Troy, and how did his adventure begin?

   Odysseus was the king of Ithaca. Because of a prophecy that he would not return for 20 years, he played crazy to avoid going to the Trojan War. His trick was exposed when he would not run a plow over his infant son Telemachus. He served well at Troy, winning the armor of Achilles. On his way home, a storm took him to the island of the lotus-eaters, the first of his adventures.

2. How did Odysseus get himself out of the following difficulties?

  a. the Cyclops: <u>After blinding the Cyclops, Odysseus and his men escaped tied to the underbellies of sheep as the Cyclops let them out of the cave to graze.</u>

  b. Circe: <u>Hermes showed Odysseus a plant to counteract the spells of Circe. Unaffected by Circe's spells, Odysseus pulled a sword on her and made her turn her victims back into men. After a year, Odysseus left the island.</u>

  c. the Sirens: <u>Odysseus made his sailors stuff their ears with wax so they would not be lured by the song of the Sirens. But wishing to hear it himself, he had himself tied to the mast with instructions that he was not to be let loose.</u>

  d. Scylla and Charybdis: <u>Seeing that he could not avoid both dangers, he steered close to Scylla to avoid the whirlpool Charybdis. The whirlpool would have taken his whole ship while Scylla only took a few sailors.</u>

3. Describe Odysseus' return to the island of Ithaca.

  <u>The sailors put the sleeping Odysseus on the beach of Ithaca. He climbed the rocks and spent the next night at the cottage of a swineherd who did not know who he was. The next morning his son Telemachus came to the cottage. Odysseus made himself known and caught up on what had been happening on the island and with his wife while he had been away.</u>

4. Describe Odysseus' return to the palace.

  <u>Over 100 suitors from Ithaca and nearby islands had been at the palace and were now pressing Penelope for a decision as to whom she would marry. Odysseus came to the palace in rags, unrecognized except by his dog. Instructed by Artemis, Penelope proposed a contest using Odysseus' bow. Only Odysseus could string and shoot it. He killed all the suitors and resumed his place as king and husband.</u>

ACTIVITIES

1. Locate on Map 7 (Odysseus' Route):
   - Ithaca
   - Strait of Messina
   - Sicily

For the teacher:
- The ancient poet of the Trojan War also composed the story of Odysseus. What is the name of this composition? *Odyssey.*
- Have your students buy, check out, or download a copy of this story. Have them read as much of it as they can. It is a good story—in fact, the original "good story." Have them pick one of Odysseus' adventures and retell it as if it were happening to them.

LESSON 12: *Lycurgus (Λυκοῦργος)*

FACTS TO KNOW

1. **Spartans** – descendants of Hercules; conquered southern Greece
2. **Helots** – conquered people forced into serfdom by the Spartans
3. **Lycurgus** – prince of Sparta; reformed the laws

"Bring up this child for Sparta." – **order of Sparta**

"Come back with this or upon this." – **saying of Spartan mothers**

"Sparta's citizens are her walls." – **Lycurgus**

VOCABULARY

1. **oligarchy** _____ government by a few persons or families _____
2. hurling **javelins** _____ throwing spears _____
3. The clothing … was **scanty**. _____ barely sufficient or adequate _____
4. **rushes** instead of a mattress. _____ stiff marsh plants; stems of same _____
5. To teach the boys **temperance** _____ abstinence from alcohol _____
6. endure pain without **flinching** [flinch] ___ to recoil involuntarily, from surprise or pain ___
7. weak and **effeminate**. _____ weak and soft in attitude and behavior _____
8. a nation of **idlers** _____ unemployed and lazy persons _____
9. **spartan** _____ frugal and self-disciplined _____

COMPREHENSION QUESTIONS

1. Describe the government and class system of Sparta.

   Sparta was an oligarchy ruled by a few families, traditionally claiming descent from

   Hercules. There were three classes—the oligarchs who were the only citizens, the

   Helot serfs consisting of people from cities conquered by Sparta, and a class of

   people neither serf nor citizen consisting of free farmers, traders, and mechanics, who

   paid taxes and fought in Sparta's wars.

2. Describe Lycurgus' laws and reforms with respect to the following:

a. the vote: _____ All citizens were given a vote. The Senate proposed laws, but enacting them required a majority vote of the assembled citizens.

b. division of land and labor: _____ Land was divided equally among citizens, as were the slaves needed to work the land.

c. money: _____ Money was made of iron to discourage import-export trade and speculation, so that no Spartan could become wealthy.

d. training: _____ Boys were required to train in running, boxing, wrestling, quoits, javelin throwing, and bow and arrow. Girls also were required to train in athletics.

e. dining: _____ Private dining was not allowed. All citizens had to dine at public tables and were served simple meals consisting mainly of bread, cheese, and the famous Spartan black soup.

3. Describe the training of Spartan boys.

At the age of seven, boys were removed from the home and trained by the state. They were given scanty clothing, and no head or foot gear. They slept on hard beds or on the floor with mattresses of rushes. They were given lessons in temperance and enduring pain. They were taught never to surrender.

ACTIVITIES

1. Locate on Maps 2, 3:
   - Peloponnesus
   - Sparta

For the teacher:
- What is the American version of the game of quoits? Have you ever played this game? If not, set up a pitch and give it a try. Horseshoes.
- One of Lycurgus' acts was to convince the rich men of Sparta to let their land be shared out among the citizens. This must not have been easy. Take the role of Lycurgus, and let another take the role of the wealthy Spartan land baron. How would you argue your case? How would you convince the rich landowner that a more equitable distribution of land is in his interests?

LESSON 13: *Draco and Solon (Δράκων and Σόλων)*

FACTS TO KNOW

1. **Draco** – began the reform of the laws of Athens
2. **Solon** – further reformed the laws of Athens
3. **archon** – ruling magistrate of Athens
4. **Crœsus** – rich king of Lydia

"Who is the happiest man you have ever known?" – **Crœsus**

"I call no man happy until he is dead. When I hear whether or not your life has ended nobly, then I shall know whether or not you were really happy." – **Solon**

VOCABULARY

1. archons were like **aldermen** [**alderman**].

   members of a city legislature

2. the lands … were **mortgaged** [**mortgage**].

   to pledge property as security for repayment of debt (loan)

COMPREHENSION QUESTIONS

1. What were the main problems with the laws of Athens prior to Draco's reforms?

   Justice was only for the rich; judges almost always decided cases in favor of their rich

   friends. Laws were too severe; many minor infractions were punished by death. Laws

   were unwritten.

2. Which laws of Athens were still unfair after Draco's reforms?

   Draco did not reform laws relating to debt. A lender could take possession of a debtor's

   house and farm for non-payment, and could sell his wife and children into slavery. A

   mortgaged property was marked by a stone pillar; Athens was thick with them.

3. What were the features of Solon's reforms, called a "shaking off of burdens"?

Solon figured that years and even generations of interest were enough. Debts of those who had lost everything were forgiven; houses and farms were returned to their owners; all who had been sold into slavery were freed; debts of those who had not lost everything were reduced by a quarter.

4. How did Solon reform the government of Athens?

Solon gave every citizen a vote. Laws were proposed by the Senate of Four Hundred but were passed by an open assembly of voting citizens (which met in the open air beneath the Acropolis). Every nine years, citizens elected archons as their rulers.

5. Contrast Solon's and Crœsus' idea of a happy man.

Crœsus equated happiness with wealth. Solon believed true happiness lay in living nobly, raising a family without suffering want, and fighting for one's country.

ACTIVITIES

1. Locate on Map 1:
   - Athens
   - Lydia
   - Asia Minor
2. Continue filling in the timeline of ancient Greece. Add the key dates through Solon.

For the teacher:
Although Draco eased the criminal laws somewhat, his laws on property and money, especially as they applied to the poor (the bulk of the population), were so severe that his name became synonymous for an exceedingly harsh measure of any kind. What is this term? Have your students come up with a couple of examples from their own experience.
The term is "draconian."

LESSON 14: *Pisistratus (Πεισίστρατος) the Tyrant*

FACTS TO KNOW

1. **Pisistratus** – seized the Acropolis; made himself tyrant of Athens
2. **Acropolis** – citadel of Athens
3. *Iliad* – Homer's epic about the Trojan War
4. *Odyssey* – Homer's epic about the wanderings of Odysseus

*"Men of Athens! See what my enemies have done to me because
I am a friend of the people."* – **Pisistratus**

VOCABULARY

1. the **citadel** of Athens _____ a city fortress in a commanding position
2. all the states ... had become **republics**. cities ruled by magistrates (citizens) instead of kings
3. **tyrant** (ancient meaning) _____ sole ruler in a Greek city republic
4. **tyrant** (modern meaning) _____ harsh and domineering person or ruler
5. Traveling **minstrels** sang them _____ itinerant (traveling) musician-poets

COMPREHENSION QUESTIONS

1. How did Pisistratus first gain power in Athens?

   After gaining the favor of the majority of the people, he staged an attack on himself.

   He then persuaded the Assembly to authorize him a body of guards, with which he

   then seized the Acropolis and took sole power.

2. List what he did to gain favor with the people.

   He gave money, opened his gardens to the men and families of the working class,

   made food for the sick from his own kitchen, sent snow to the ill in summer, and paid

   burial expenses for the poor.

3. How did he regain power after being deposed?

He entered the city in a chariot with a tall beautiful girl in full armor at his side. This bit of theater was meant to imply that Athena herself was bringing Pisistratus back to rule the city.

4. Name three good things Pisistratus did for Athens.

He put all the marketplace idlers to work on public projects, he established a large library for everyone, and he commissioned the writing of manuscripts of the epics of Homer.

For the teacher:

- Have your students draw a map of the Acropolis, to include the primary structures (examples may be found online or at a library with a good ancient history section).

- Have your students sketch on paper, create graphically on a computer, or verbally describe the Parthenon. What two major structural elements are now missing?
  Missing are most of the inner sanctum and the roof. Only the outer colonnade is more or less complete.

- What are the Elgin marbles? Why are they called by this name, and where are they now located? Where were they originally located? What is the controversy that now surrounds them?
  The Elgin marbles are the marble sculptures originally arrayed around the tops of the inner and outer colonnades and the pediments of the Parthenon. About half of them were removed to London (British Museum) beginning in 1801 by Lord Elgin, British ambassador to the Ottoman Empire (that ruled Greece at the time) under a grant from the Sultan. The Greeks are demanding that they be returned.

LESSON 15: *Miltiades (Μιλτιάδης), the Hero of Marathon*

FACTS TO KNOW

1. **Hippias** – son of Pisistratus; ruled Athens until driven out for cruelty

2. **Hipparchus** – son of Pisistratus; ruled Athens with his brother until killed by enemies

3. **Darius I ("the Great")** – king of Persia

4. **Miltiades** – Greek general; victor of the battle of Marathon

5. **Phidippides** – messenger who ran 22 miles to announce the victory of Marathon

6. **Theseus** – hero-god said to have fought for the Greeks at Marathon

"There you will find both earth and water for your master." – **the Spartans**

"Rejoice! Rejoice! We are victors!" – **Phidippides**

VOCABULARY

1. Persian **heralds** were sent _messengers delivering important news_

2. They had **routed** [**rout**] an army _to drive off in disorder_

3. **havoc** among the Persians. _chaos and disorder_

4. **marathon** _a cross-country foot race of 26.2 miles_

COMPREHENSION QUESTIONS

1. Why did Persian agents show up in Greek cities demanding a tribute of earth and water? What did this demand mean and how was it received?

   After being driven from Athens, Hippias went to Darius, king of Persia, for assistance in retaking power. Darius saw this as an opportunity to take power over all of Greece himself. His agents' demand of a tribute of earth and water implied that, if given, Darius would be the rightful ruler of the city. The Spartans threw the agents into a well, saying, "Here's your earth and water."

2. Describe the opposing armies at Marathon, the strategy of Miltiades, and the outcome.

   The Persians landed with 150,000 men and set up camp at Marathon. The Athenians had only 10,000 under 10 rotating generals. Their best general was Miltiades, whose strategy was an immediate frontal attack. He charged the Persian front line. His speed and boldness broke the Persians, who retreated to their ships.

3. Describe how the news of the victory was received at Athens, and the follow-up.

Most Athenians naturally rejoiced at the news. A few traitors, however, signaled the

Persian fleet to attack Athens before Miltiades could return. But Miltiades saw the

signal and sped back to Athens, preventing a landing and attack by the Persians, who

went back to Persia.

4. How did the Athenians get the news of the Greek victory over the Persians so quickly?

Phidippides, a Greek soldier, ran the 22 miles from Marathon to Athens to deliver the

news. Then he collapsed and died.

5. How did Miltiades destroy his own legend?

He asked for and was given a fleet of 70 ships with which he attacked the island of

Paros, both for having supported the Persians and also to settle a personal score.

The expedition was a complete failure and Miltiades was injured. Miltiades was

indicted for deception and wasting public money. He was fined heavily and soon died

of his injuries.

6. How did the Athenians remember him and restore him to honor?

The Athenians chose to remember Miltiades for Marathon, not Paros, and buried him

with highest honors in the Marathon plain.

ACTIVITIES

1. Locate on Maps 1, 2:
   - Paros
   - Plataea
   - plain of Marathon
   - Aegean Sea
2. Continue filling in the timeline of ancient Greece. Add the key dates through Marathon.

For the teacher:
Have your students do their own research and mark out the approximate extent of the Persian Empire
at the time of Darius the Great. You may use a copy of Map 9 or any other map of the appropriate
region. Online, search: Darius, Persian Empire.

REVIEW LESSON 3: *Lessons 11-15*

IMPORTANT DATES: *See Timeline.*

c. 1200 B.C.	**1.**	Trojan War
490 B.C.	**2.**	battle of Marathon

THINGS TO KNOW

Scylla and Charybdis	**1.**	monster of the Strait of Messina and deadly whirlpool
Æolus	**2.**	god of the winds
Circe	**3.**	sorceress who turned men into animals
Cyclops	**4.**	one-eyed giant
Calypso	**5.**	sea-nymph who cared for Odysseus
Helots	**6.**	conquered people made serfs by the Spartans
archon	**7.**	magistrate of Athens
Acropolis	**8.**	citadel of Athens
Iliad	**9.**	epic about the Trojan War
Odyssey	**10.**	epic about the adventures of one of its heroes
Nausicaa	**11.**	island princess; found Odysseus on the shore

IMPORTANT PEOPLE

Odysseus	**1.**	king of Ithaca; hero of the Trojan War
Telemachus	**2.**	son of Odysseus
Penelope	**3.**	wife of Odysseus
Lycurgus	**4.**	reformed the laws of Sparta
Draco	**5.**	began the reform of the laws of Athens
Solon	**6.**	completed the reform of the laws of Athens
Crœsus	**7.**	rich king of Lydia
Pisistratus	**8.**	good tyrant of Athens
Miltiades	**9.**	victor at Marathon
Phidippides	**10.**	messenger who ran from Marathon to Athens to announce victory
Darius I	**11.**	king of Persia

WHO SAID THAT?

1. "I care nothing for gods! But as for men, let me show you how much I like them!" ___Cyclops___

2. "Loose me! Loose me! I must go nearer that music!" ___Odysseus___

3. "Come back with this or on this." ___Spartan mothers___

4. "Sparta's citizens are her walls." ___Lycurgus___

5. "I call no man happy until he is dead. When I hear whether or not your life has ended nobly, then I shall know whether or not you were really happy." ___Solon___

6. "See what my enemies have done to me because I am a friend of the people." ___Pisistratus___

7. "There you will find both earth and water for your master." ___the Spartans___

8. "Rejoice! Rejoice! We are victors!" ___Phidippides___

COMPREHENSION QUESTIONS TO REVIEW

1. Describe Odysseus' return to his palace.

   Over 100 suitors from Ithaca and nearby islands had been at the palace and were now pressing Penelope for a decision. Odysseus came to the palace in rags, unrecognized except by his dog. Instructed by Athena, Penelope proposed a contest using Odysseus' bow. Only Odysseus could string and shoot it. He killed all the suitors and resumed his place as king and husband.

2. Describe the government and class system of Sparta.

   Sparta was an oligarchy ruled by a few families, traditionally claiming descent from Hercules. There were three classes: the oligarchs who were the only citizens, the Helot serfs consisting of people from cities conquered by Sparta, and a class of people neither serf nor citizen consisting of free farmers, traders, and mechanics, who paid taxes and fought in Sparta's wars.

3. What good things did Pisistratus do for Athens?

   He put all the marketplace idlers to work on public projects, he established a large library for everyone, and he commissioned the writing of manuscripts of the epics of Homer.

4. Describe Solon's "shaking off of burdens."

Solon figured that years and even generations of interest were enough. Debts of those who had lost everything were forgiven; houses and farms were returned to their owners; all who had been sold into slavery were freed; debts of those who had not lost everything were reduced by a quarter.

5. How was the news of the victory at Marathon received in Athens, and what happened afterward?

Most Athenians naturally rejoiced at the news. A few traitors, however, signaled the Persian fleet to attack Athens before Miltiades could return. But Miltiades saw the signal and sped back to Athens, preventing a landing and attack by the Persians, who went back to Persia.

VOCABULARY

idler	to rout	alderman	temperance	rushes	mortgage	flinch
spartan	shroud	haughty	republic	squall	stately	cavern
to low	scanty	herald	havoc	javelin	effeminate	odyssey
citadel	tyrant	minstrel	oligarchy	marathon	lotus	

__flinch__   1. to recoil involuntarily

__cavern__   2. large cave

__haughty__   3. scornfully proud

__minstrel__   4. itinerant musician-poet

__havoc__   5. chaos and disorder

__scanty__   6. barely sufficient or adequate

__squall__   7. a sudden, brief, violent storm

__republic__   8. city ruled by magistrates instead of kings

__alderman__   9. member of a municipal legislature

__herald__   10. messenger delivering important news

__spartan__   11. frugal and self-disciplined

__javelin__   12. a throwing spear

__stately__   13. majestic and dignified

__tyrant__   14. oppressive and arbitrary person

__rout__   15. to drive off in disorder

__temperance__   16. abstinence from alcohol

__lotus__   17. fruit that induces forgetfulness

__idler__   18. a lazy person

__citadel__   19. a city fortress in a commanding position

__rushes__   20. stiff marsh plants

__odyssey__   21. a long adventurous voyage

__effeminate__   22. weak and soft in attitude or behavior

__tyrant__   23. sole ruler of a Greek city republic

__marathon__   24. a cross-country foot race of 26.2 miles

__shroud__   25. a burial cloth

__oligarchy__   26. government by the few

__low__   27. to moo

__mortgage__   28. to pledge property as security for repayment of debt (loan)

GEOGRAPHY REVIEW: *Study the location of the following places.*

Countries, Islands
- Sicily
- Asia Minor

Cities
- Sparta
- Athens
- Marathon

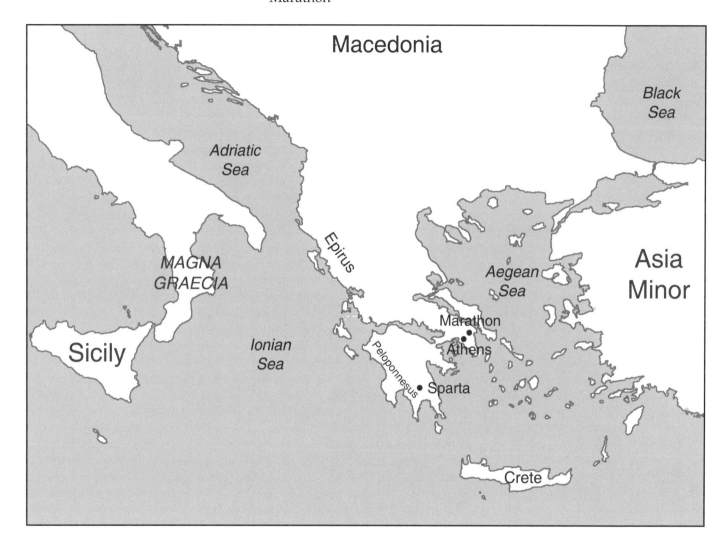

GEOGRAPHY REVIEW: *Use the following places to complete the maps.*

Countries, Islands
- Sicily
- Asia Minor

Cities
- Sparta
- Athens
- Marathon

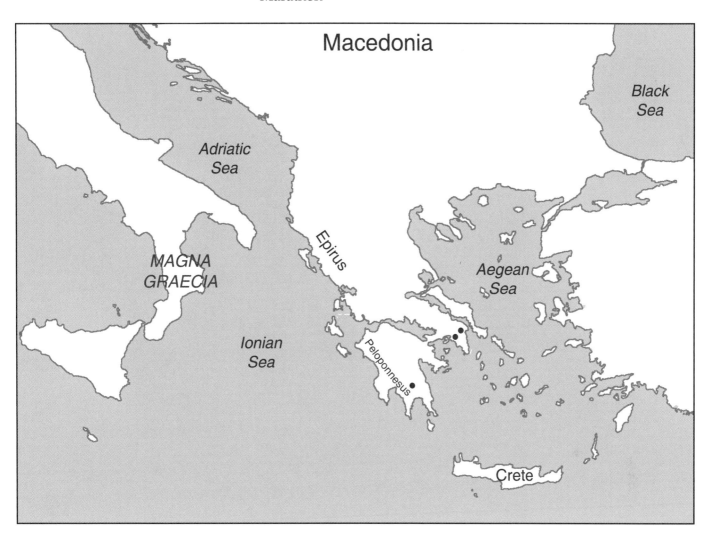

Drawing Page

Drawing Page

LESSON 16: *Leonidas (Λεωνίδας) at Thermopylæ*

FACTS TO KNOW

1. **Leonidas** – king of Sparta; hero of Thermopylæ
2. **Xerxes** – king of Persia; succeeded Darius I, his father
3. **Pass of Thermopylæ** – site of the heroic stand of Leonidas' 4,000 men against the army of Xerxes in 480 B.C.

"So much the better, we shall fight in the shade." – **Spartan soldier at Thermopylæ**

"Stranger, tell the Spartans that we lie here in obedience to their commands." – **inscription on the Spartan memorial**

VOCABULARY

1. hot **sulphur** springs _____ a yellow mineral*
2. **scourged** [**scourge**] with ... lashes _____ to beat with a small whip as punishment
3. impossible to **scale**. _____ to climb in stages or on a ladder

*associated with volcanoes and not springs; considered to have healing powers

COMPREHENSION QUESTIONS

1. Why did Xerxes have the sea scourged?

   After witnessing the destruction of his pontoon bridges across the Hellespont in a

   storm, Xerxes had his agents beat the sea and throw chains into it to teach the water

   that he was its master. In practical terms, this was a demonstration to his men and

   engineers that they could and would bridge the strait.

   _____

   _____

   _____

2. Describe the combined forces of Xerxes.

   Xerxes spent four years collecting his forces. He had a fleet of 1,200 war ships and

   3,000 smaller vessels. His combined fleet and army were the largest ever assembled.

   It took the army seven days and nights to cross the bridge.

   _____

   _____

   _____

   _____

3. Why was the stand of the Spartans at Thermopylæ especially heroic?

For two days Leonidas and his band of 300 Spartans had held the pass against

thousands of Persians. When a traitor showed the Persians a route to the rear,

Leonidas had time to escape, but chose to stand and fight.

4. What was the outcome of Xerxes' invasion?

Xerxes found Athens almost deserted. His men found an undefended place to cross

over the wall. The Athenians who had stayed to defend the city either committed

suicide or were killed. The Persians plundered and burned the city.

ACTIVITIES

1. Locate on Maps 1, 3:
   - Sardis
   - Hellespont (Dardanelles)
   - Pass of Thermopylae

For the teacher:
Have your students review Lesson 7 on Jason and the Golden Fleece. Have them tell the story of how the Hellespont got its name, making sure to tell how this story is related to Jason's adventure.

A Grecian king was told by an oracle that Zeus wanted him to sacrifice his son Phrixus. As Phrixus awaited the knife, a ram with a fleece of gold appeared. Phrixus and his sister Helle jumped onto the ram and fled. When they got to the first of two straits that connects the Ægean Sea with the Black Sea, Phrixus and Helle attempted to swim across. He made it, but she drowned, and the strait was named Hellespont (Helle's Sea) after her.

LESSON 17: *Themistocles (Θεμιστοκλῆς)*

FACTS TO KNOW

1. **Themistocles** – Athenian statesman and soldier; advised the Athenians to build more ships
2. **oracle of Delphi** – main oracle of the Athenian domain
3. **Pythia** – priestess of the oracle
4. **battle of Salamis** – naval battle where the Athenians defeated the Persians

"We fight for all." – **the Greeks at Salamis**

VOCABULARY

1. **tripod** ___three-legged stand or stool___
2. the narrow **strait** of Salamis ___narrow passage of water between two shores___
3. **banished** [banish] from Athens. ___to expel and send away as punishment___

COMPREHENSION QUESTIONS

1. Describe the oracle of Delphi and the procedure for consulting it.
   Delphi was on the slopes of Mt. Parnassus. The inner chamber of the shrine was
   built over a cleft in the rock. A three-legged stool was over the cleft. The priestess
   took her seat on this stool. She would go into a trance and speak prophecy. It was
   believed that Apollo spoke through her, but it is now thought that she experienced the
   intoxicating effect of fumes escaping from the rock.

2. How did Themistocles interpret the oracle's prophecy regarding Xerxes?
   The priestess spoke of a "wooden wall," which Themistocles interpreted to be a wall
   of ships. He encouraged the Athenians to build more ships and prepare for a great
   sea battle.

3. Why did Themistocles betray the Athenians' escape and other Greek leaders to Xerxes?

Themistocles knew that the best way to equalize the difference in size between his navy and the larger Persian fleet was to fight in the strait. The Greek leaders did not understand this and planned to escape. Themistocles thwarted this by betraying their plans to Xerxes.

4. Describe the fleets of the Persians and the Greeks.

The Persians had 1,000 vessels and the Greeks had less than 400. These vessels were galleys with up to 150 oars. The Greeks, however, were the better seamen.

5. How did the Greeks win the battle of Salamis?

The Greeks chose to fight in the strait after Themistocles effectively prevented their retreat. This caused confusion and havoc in the large Persian fleet, whose ships were ramming each other or preventing them from fighting effectively. The Greeks destroyed 200 Persian ships with the loss of only 40 of their own.

ACTIVITIES

1. Locate on Map 2:
   - Delphi
   - Salamis
   - Attica
   - Argos

For the teacher:

- Greek warships are called "gigantic rowboats" in the text, but this name is inappropriate. The generic name for this type of ship is "galley." It is propelled by rowers sitting on one or multiple decks pulling huge oars. These ships were capable of 20 knots in spurts, were quite maneuverable, were equipped with rams, and were formidable weapons of war—hardly rowboats. Galleys were used in naval warfare till the 1500s.

- Have your students find a good illustration of an ancient Greek war galley and sketch their own version. Online, search: galley. A site with some good images, available at the time of this printing, is: https://www.scienceandsociety.co.uk/results.asp?txtkeys1=Galleys

LESSON 18: *Aristides (Ἀριστείδης) the Just*

FACTS TO KNOW

1. **Aristides** – Athenian magistrate and general; rival of Themistocles; had a reputation for fairness
2. **Mardonius** – Persian general; left in command of the Persian forces in Thessaly after Xerxes' retreat
3. **Pausanias** – nephew of Leonidas; defeated Mardonius at Platæa
4. **battle of Mycale** – last sea battle between the Greeks and the Persians
5. **battle of Platæa** – last land battle fought between Greeks and Persians in 479 B.C. (fought on same day as battle of Mycale)

"I have never seen him but I am tired of hearing him called 'the Just.'" – **Athenian to Aristides**

VOCABULARY

1. **ostracism** (ancient meaning) _____temporary banishment by popular vote_____
2. **ostracism** (modern meaning)_____exclusion from a group, possibly for some disgrace_____

COMPREHENSION QUESTIONS

1. What were the similarities and differences of character between Themistocles and Aristides?
   Both were wise and brave, but Themistocles was selfish and fond of money, while Aristides was honorable and fair.

2. What was ostracism and how did it work?
   Once a year citizens were asked if the state was endangered by any individual among them. A vote was taken in the form of names written anonymously on small clay pieces. If any man collected over 6,000 votes, he was obliged to leave the city for ten years. He could, however, be recalled.

3. How was Aristides banished, and why was he recalled?
   At the instigation of Themistocles, a popular dislike of Aristides was created to the degree that Aristides was banished, which he accepted gracefully. In the emergence that came to a head at Salamis, Themistocles himself, at the urging of the citizens, recalled Aristides. Aristides was put in command of a ship and performed well.

4. Describe the battle of Platæa, the division of the spoils, and the victory offerings.

After capturing an undefended Athens, Mardonius was met in battle at Platæa by 110,000 Greeks under Pausanias. Aristides was put in field command of the troops. Mardonius was defeated and killed. It took ten days to divide the spoils and bury the dead. A tenth of the spoils was sent to Delphi as an offering to Apollo. Liberty games every fourth year were begun at the battlefield, which was declared sacred.

5. What did the Athenians do after the victories of Platæa and Mycale?

After these victories, the Athenians returned to their city and began energetically to rebuild it. Aristides and Themistocles worked together on it. The port of Piræus was fortified and a wall was built around Athens. Aristides was in charge of the funds raised for the project.

ACTIVITIES

1. Locate on Maps 1-3:
- Thessaly
- Plataea
- Mycale
- Asia Minor

LESSON 19: *Cimon (Κίμων)*

FACTS TO KNOW

1. **Cimon** – son of Miltiades
2. **Æschylus** – Greek dramatist
3. **Sophocles** – Greek dramatist
4. **Long Walls** – walls connecting Athens with the port of Piræus
5. **Aristophanes** – Greek comic playwright

"Athens and Sparta are the two legs of Greece." – **Cimon**

"Because Cimon is already with me." – **oracle of Zeus**

VOCABULARY

1. took so much **booty** from pirates ___plunder___
2. suffer Greece to be **maimed** [**maim**] ___to disable or disfigure___
3. the "Great King's" **dominions**. ___realms; territories ruled by someone___

COMPREHENSION QUESTIONS

1. Why did Cimon hang up his bridle?

   Cimon, a member of the class of knights, hung up his bridle in the temple of Athena to express the idea that at the time Athens needed seamen, not horsemen.

2. What did Cimon do on Scyros, and what did he find there?

   Cimon captured the island of Scyros, the pirates that had their base there, and their vessels. He found the bones of the hero Theseus and brought them to Athens.

3. How did Cimon build the Athenian navy, what were his first victories, and what was the agreement he forced on the Persian king?

When the allies of Athens grew tired of warfare, Cimon encouraged them to furnish ships and money. He hired sailors from among the Athenians, drilled them in naval warfare, and took them on several expeditions. He defeated two Persian fleets and a Persian army on land, forcing the Persian king to again agree never to enter the Ægean or come nearer than 50 miles on land.

4. For what were the spoils taken from the war with the Persians used?

A portion of the spoils of the war were used to build the Long Walls connecting Athens to Piræus, providing fortification from Athens to the sea.

5. Why did Sparta ask Athens for troops? Why did Cimon agree to send them?

Sparta came to Athens for help because in the chaos following an earthquake, their Helots had risen in revolt. Neighboring cities had joined the revolt. As Athens and Sparta were rivals, some in Athens opposed giving aid to Sparta, but Cimon was in favor because of the mutual interest of the two cities in putting down the revolt.

6. How did this result in the banishment of Cimon, and why was Cimon recalled?

The action failed, Sparta rejected further Athenian support, and Athens banished Cimon as a friend of Sparta. The Spartans did put down the revolt and then sent an army against Athens. Cimon was recalled as a general who could either defeat the Spartans or make friends with them as the occasion required.

ACTIVITIES

1. Locate on Maps 1, 2:
   - Scyros
   - Aegean Sea
   - Athens
   - Piraeus
   - Sparta

LESSON 20: *Pericles* (Περικλῆς)

FACTS TO KNOW

1. **Pericles** – leader of Athens at the beginning of the Peloponnesian War
2. **Peloponnesian War** – 431-404 B.C.; war between Athens and Sparta that destroyed the Athenian empire
3. **Phidias** – Greek sculptor; made Parthenon statuary
4. **Parthenon** – temple and treasury on the Acropolis of Athens
5. **Herodotus** – Greek historian; "father of history"; wrote a history of the Persian wars
6. **Thucydides** – Greek historian; wrote a history of the Peloponnesian War

"What you praise in my life has been due to fortune. I deserve no credit for it." – **Pericles**

"That of which I am proudest is that no Athenian ever wore mourning
because of anything done by me." – **Pericles**

VOCABULARY

1. a contest that **desolated** [**desolate**] Greece ___to lay waste; to destroy; to make unfit for habitation___
2. This was the **plague**. ___highly infectious, usually fatal epidemic disease___
3. across the **Isthmus** of Corinth ___strip of land connecting two larger masses of land___

COMPREHENSION QUESTIONS

1. What are the important laws of Pericles?
   Pericles established the right of a citizen to be tried by a certain number of his fellow citizens. He proposed pay for members of the armed forces and free theater tickets for the poor.

2. What are the most important construction projects of Pericles?
   Pericles finished the Long Walls and commissioned the Parthenon on the Acropolis.

3. What strategy did Pericles use when Athens was under attack by the Spartans, and what was its effect?

Pericles' strategy was to concentrate the citizens of the countryside around Athens inside the city itself. Athens was the best fortified city in Greece at the time. But when plague hit the city, the concentration of people inside made the death toll very high and contributed to the eventual defeat of Athens in the war.

4. Name some of the artists and authors active in Athens under Pericles.

The sculptor Phidias, the historians Herodotus, and Thucydides.

ACTIVITIES

1. Locate on Maps 2, 3:
   - Corcyra (Corfu)
   - Corinth
   - Isthmus of Corinth
   - Attica
   - Peloponnesus

2. Update the timeline of ancient Greece through Pericles.

For the teacher:
Have your students go online or to a library and find a copy of Pericles' Funeral Oration. Have them read it and report on it. It is fairly short. Online, search: Pericles' Funeral Oration.

REVIEW LESSON 4: *Lessons 16-20*

IMPORTANT DATES: *See Timeline*

490 B.C.		**1.**	battle of Marathon
480 B.C.		**2.**	battles of Thermopylæ and Salamis
479 B.C.		**3.**	battle of Platæa
431-404 B.C.		**4.**	Peloponnesian War

IMPORTANT PEOPLE

Leonidas		**1.**	hero of Thermopylæ and king of Sparta
Xerxes		**2.**	king of Persia after Darius I, his father
Themistocles		**3.**	advised the Athenians to build more ships
Aristides		**4.**	Athenian magistrate and general
Cimon		**5.**	son of Miltiades who defeated the Persians
Pericles		**6.**	dominant Athenian leader at the start of the Peloponnesian War
Herodotus		**7.**	wrote a history of the Persian wars
Thucydides		**8.**	wrote a history of the Peloponnesian War
Phidias		**9.**	Greek sculptor who carved statuary for the Acropolis
Pausanias		**10.**	Greek general at Plataea
Mardonius		**11.**	Persian general killed at Plataea
Aeschylus & Sophocles		**12.**	Greek dramatists during time of Cimon
Aristophanes		**13.**	Greek comic playwright of the 5th century B.C.

THINGS TO KNOW

Pass of Thermopylæ		**1.**	site of Leonidas' stand against the army of Xerxes
oracle of Delphi		**2.**	most important oracle for the Athenians
battle of Salamis		**3.**	site of the crucial naval victory of Athenians over the Persians
Long Walls		**4.**	defensive works connecting Athens with the port of Piræus
Parthenon		**5.**	main temple on the Acropolis
Dardanelles		**6.**	modern name of the Hellespont
Corfu		**7.**	alternate name of Corcyra
Peloponnesian War		**8.**	war between Athens and Sparta

battle of Mycale	**9.** last sea battle between Persians and Greeks
battle of Plataea	**10.** last land battle between Persians and Greeks

WHO SAID THAT?

1. "So much the better, we shall fight in the shade." _Spartan soldier at Thermopylæ_

2. "We fight for all." _Greeks at Salamis_

3. "I have never seen him but I am tired of hearing him called 'the Just'." _Athenian to Aristides_

4. "Athens and Sparta are the two legs of Greece." _Cimon_

5. "What you praise in my life has been due to fortune. I deserve no credit for it." _Pericles_

6. "That of which I am proudest is that no Athenian ever wore mourning because of anything done by me."
   Pericles

COMPREHENSION QUESTIONS TO REVIEW

1. What did the army of Xerxes find when it reached Athens, and what did it do?

   Xerxes found Athens almost deserted. His men found an undefended place to cross over the wall. The Athenians who had stayed to defend the city either committed suicide or were killed. The Persians plundered and burned the city.

2. What was the Greek strategy at the battle of Salamis and what was the outcome?

   The Greeks chose to fight in the strait. This caused confusion and havoc in the large Persian fleet, whose ships were ramming each other or preventing them from fighting effectively. The Greeks destroyed 200 Persian ships with the loss of only 40 of their own.

3. Describe the battle of Platæa, the division of spoils, and the victory offerings.

   After capturing an undefended Athens, Mardonius was met in battle at Platæa by 110,000 Greeks under Pausanias. Aristides was put in field command of the troops. Mardonius was defeated and killed. It took ten days to divide the spoils and bury the dead. A tenth of the spoils was sent to Delphi as an offering to Apollo. Liberty games every fourth year were begun at the battlefield, which was declared sacred.

4. How did Cimon build the Athenian navy, what victories did he win, and what terms did he force on the Persians?

When the allies of Athens grew tired of warfare, Cimon encouraged them to furnish ships and money. He hired sailors from among the Athenians, drilled them in naval warfare, and took them on several expeditions. He defeated two Persian fleets and a Persian army on land, forcing the Persian king to again agree never to enter the Ægean or come nearer than 50 miles on land.

5. What was Pericles' strategy in dealing with the Spartan attack, and what was its effect?

Pericles' strategy was to concentrate the citizens of the countryside around Athens inside the city itself. Athens was the best fortified city in Greece at the time. But when plague hit the city, the concentration of people inside made the death toll very high and contributed to the eventual defeat of Athens in the war.

VOCABULARY

banish	strait	booty	sulphur	maim	tripod	plague
ostracism	isthmus	scourge	dominion	scale	desolate	

maim _____ **1.** to disable or disfigure

tripod _____ **2.** three-legged stand or stool

scale _____ **3.** to climb with ladders

ostracism _____ **4.** temporary banishment by popular vote

booty _____ **5.** plunder taken from an enemy in war

banish _____ **6.** to expel as punishment

scourge _____ **7.** to whip as punishment

ostracism _____ **8.** being excluded from, or ignored by, a group

dominion _____ **9.** territory ruled by someone

strait _____ **10.** narrow passage of water between two shores

sulphur _____ **11.** yellow mineral deposited around hot springs

desolate _____ **12.** to destroy; to lay waste; to make unfit for habitation

plague _____ **13.** highly infectious, usually fatal epidemic disease

isthmus _____ **14.** strip of land connecting two larger masses of land

GEOGRAPHY REVIEW: *Study the location of the following places.*

Countries, Islands
- Salamis

Cities
- Delphi
- Corinth

Bodies of Water, Mountains
- Pass of Thermopylae

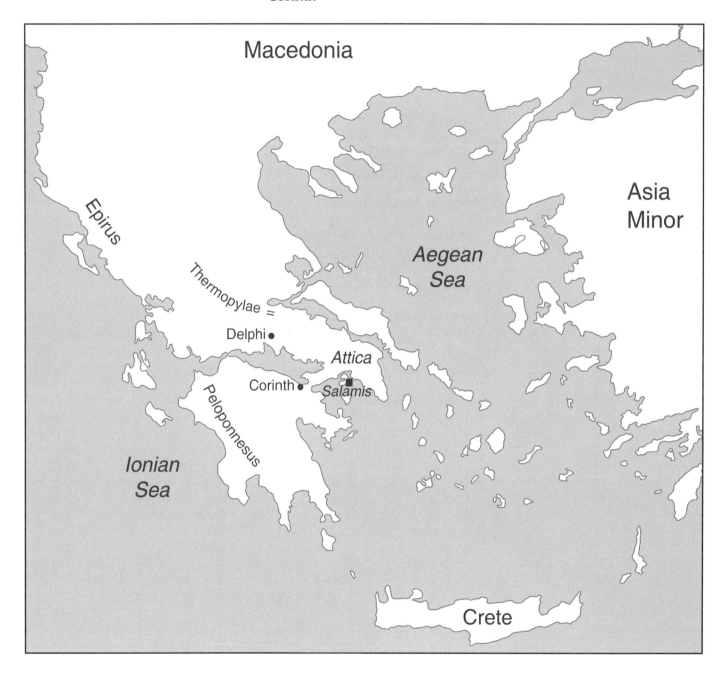

GEOGRAPHY REVIEW: *Use the following places to complete the maps.*

Countries, Islands
- Salamis

Cities
- Delphi
- Corinth

Bodies of Water, Mountains
- Pass of Thermopylae

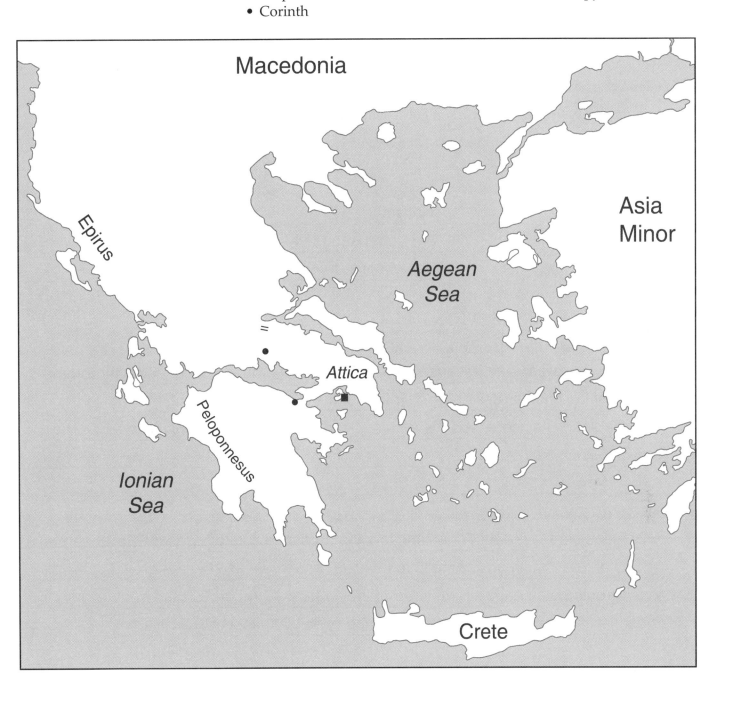

LESSON 21: *Alcibiades (Ἀλκιβιάδης)*

FACTS TO KNOW

1. **Alcibiades** – naval commander during the Peloponnesian War

2. **Olympic Games** – important athletic contest held every four years; began in Elis in 776 B.C.

3. **Nicias** – primary commander of the ill-fated Sicilian expedition

VOCABULARY

1. a **kinsman** of Pericles _____ relative _____

2. **olympiad** _____ four-year period between Olympic games _____

3. the leader of Athenian **fops**._____ men obsessed with latest fashions; dandies _____

COMPREHENSION QUESTIONS

1. Why was Alcibiades first admired by the Athenians, and what were his faults?

    Alcibiades was admired because he was rich, handsome, dashing, and a three-time winner of the chariot race at the Olympic Games. At the same time, he was vain, inconsiderate, insincere, and the de facto leader of a pack of young Athenians who sometimes caused trouble.

2. Why was the expedition to Sicily undertaken, and what was its outcome?

    Alcibiades persuaded the Athenians to send an expedition to Syracuse because it was an ally of Sparta, because Athens needed its resources, and because it was assumed that it would be an easy target. It turned out to be the greatest disaster of the war for Athens, with a total loss of a very large and expensive fleet with all its men.

3. Why was Alcibiades recalled to Athens, and how did he respond?

    Alcibiades was ordered to return to face a charge of sacrilege stemming from a defacement incident he and his buddies were suspected of being involved in prior to his departure for Sicily. He diverted to Sparta instead.

4. How did Alcibiades eventually return to Athens?

After wearing out his welcome both in Sparta and Persia, Alcibiades returned to

Athens, and with his charm got control of a fleet again. The Athenians had been

thinking they might still need him, as things had been going badly for them in the war.

5. Why was he finally dismissed from his command?

He used his fleet to attack an ally of Athens and enslave the inhabitants. He went into

exile in Asia Minor, where he was killed when his home was attacked.

ACTIVITIES

1. Locate on Maps 2, 4:
   - Olympia
   - Elis
   - Sicily
   - Syracuse

For the teacher:
Have your students do their own research and describe the ancient Olympic Games. Have them tell what kinds of sports were contested, what kinds of facilities were available, what kinds of prizes were awarded, and what the effect of Olympic victory was on the individual athletes and their cities. Online, search: Olympic games.

LESSON 22: *Lysander (Λύσανδρος)*

FACTS TO KNOW

1. **Lysander** – Spartan admiral at the end of the Peloponnesian War; captured Athens
2. **Thirty Tyrants** – governors of defeated Athens, installed by Sparta
3. **Thrasybulus** – Athenian who overthrew the Tyrants

"When the lion's skin is too short, you must patch it with that of a fox." – **Lysander**

VOCABULARY

1. He was brave but also **cunning** ___showing artful deception or trickery___

COMPREHENSION QUESTIONS

1. How was Lysander a fox against the Athenian fleet at Ægos Potamos?

   Lysander lined up his ships as if ready to give battle, but when the Athenians approached, he did nothing. He repeated this performance for four days until the Athenians, assuming he was afraid, let their guard down. At this point, Lysander moved in and captured almost the entire Athenian fleet.

2. What was the outcome of this battle, and what was its effect on Athens?

   This was the end for Athens. Lysander brought his fleet to Piræus and blocked all the Athenian ports. He cut off the food to the city.

3. What finally caused Athens to surrender and admit defeat in the Peloponnesian War?

   After three months of siege, famine was so severe in Athens that they finally gave up.

4. What terms did Sparta impose on Athens?

   Sparta required the destruction of a long segment of the Long Walls, which had always been a sore point in the conflict. Athens was to have no more than twelve warships and the Spartans appointed governors for the city. Only 3,000 Athenians were allowed to live in Athens, and all other Grecian cities were forbidden to offer refuge to the displaced citizens.

5. What prevented Lysander from seizing the Spartan throne?

He was killed in an expedition against Thebes, which had offered refuge to the displaced Athenians against Sparta's orders.

6. What was the overall effect of the Peloponnesian War?

The war was devastating to Greece as a whole. The old Athenian maritime empire was finished for good, as was its style of democracy. (Sparta was exhausted and unable to capitalize on its victory. The power of Thebes temporarily increased. This conflict set the stage for Alexander and then the conquest of Greece by the Romans and the end of Greek independence for two millennia.)

ACTIVITIES

1. Locate on Maps 1, 2:
   - Hellespont
   - Thebes
   - Aegos Potamos
   - Argos

For the teacher:

The Peloponnesian War was an event that changed history. Its effects can be followed to the present time. In general terms, what was the political nature of the Greek world before the war and after it?
The Peloponnesian War brought an end to the era of city-states and the loose-knit federations of these small powers. By exhausting Athens and Sparta, the war set the stage for the age of empires—the Macedonian Empire followed by the Roman Empire. This was the age of superpowers, strong rulers, huge armies, and navies.

LESSON 23: *Socrates (Σωκράτης)*

FACTS TO KNOW

1. **Socrates** – Athenian teacher and philosopher
2. **Socratic method*** – Socrates' question-and-answer method of teaching
3. **Xanthippe** – wife of Socrates
4. **Plato** – philosopher; pupil of Socrates; carried on Socrates' work and wrote Socrates' teachings
5. **Academy** – Plato's open-air school at Athens

"What! Would you have me die guilty?" – **Socrates**

"You can bury my body; you cannot put me into a grave." – **Socrates**

*"My judges, you go now to your homes, I to prison and to death. But which
of the two is the better lot, God only knows."* – **Socrates**

*"Thus died the man who was in death the noblest we have ever
known, in life, the wisest and the best."* – **Plato**

VOCABULARY

1. to drink the deadly juice of … **hemlock**. poisonous plant used for executions in ancient Greece
2. what the Greeks called "**philosophy**." the love and pursuit of wisdom
3. which of the two is the better **lot** fortune; choice

COMPREHENSION QUESTIONS

1. What were the two kinds of training Socrates experienced as a young person? What might he have learned from each that would benefit a philosopher?

    As an apprentice sculptor, Socrates would have learned about the Greek ideals of artistic beauty. As a soldier, he would have learned to bear hardship with equanimity and to accept fate.

2. Describe Socrates' school and his way of teaching.

    Socrates had no schoolhouse but taught in the open air (many schools in the ancient world were open-air) to whomever wished to attend. In summer, he would go to the port of Athens (Piræus) to teach. His way of teaching was oral, through telling stories of philosophy (and the question-and-answer technique now known as the Socratic method).

---

*Not covered in the textbook.

3. How did Socrates make enemies and on what charges was he officially indicted?

As one who fearlessly exposed the contradictions and foolishness of unconsidered thought and action, Socrates must have occasionally aroused irritation, discomfiture, and anger in those around him. In a conservative society, Socrates' freedom to question tradition and devotion to the gods was a threat to society as people knew it— and it scared them. Socrates was accused of leading the young astray and insulting the gods. What these charges actually meant was that he was considered a danger to the state.

4. How was Socrates as much an example by his death as by his life?

Socrates accepted his sentence gracefully and did not protest his innocence. He did not condemn his accusers or executioner. He used the month grace period he was given to commune with his friends and continue teaching. He taught that death is a passage to a nobler existence. He remained cheerful to the end.

5. How was the work of Socrates carried on so that we know about it today?

Socrates' pupil, Plato, carried on his teaching and wrote several books on the philosophy of Socrates. These books survived because they were considered fundamental to education. The points and questions contained in Plato's books have been addressed in one way or another by virtually every philosopher since.

ACTIVITIES

1. Locate on Maps 1, 3:
   - Athens
   - Thrace
   - Delos

For the teacher:

- Have your students try this exercise:
  Pair off with a fellow student. Think of an abstract idea that you will attempt to communicate to the other person. The thing is, you cannot simply state the idea. You must convey it only by asking questions and getting answers. See if you can communicate your idea in this way.

- Have your students make a short list of some of Plato's works. Online, search: Plato.

LESSON 24: *Xenophon (Ξενοφῶν)*

FACTS TO KNOW

1. **Xenophon** – Greek general; author of the history, *Anabasis*

2. **Artaxerxes** – Persian king

3. **Cyrus** – Persian general; brother of Artaxerxes

4. *Anabasis* – "The March Upcountry" or "The March of the Ten Thousand"; Xenophon's history of Cyrus' march toward Babylon and the retreat of the Greek "ten thousand"

"Victory!" – **the Greeks at the battle of Cunaxa**

"I see the man." – **Cyrus**

"And where can the good and the noble be found?" – **Socrates**

VOCABULARY

1. The Greeks were now in a terrible **plight**. difficulty; hardship

2. the **sentries** listened   guards

COMPREHENSION QUESTIONS

1. Why did Xenophon go to Persia, how did he decide to go, and what had he been doing at the time?

   Xenophon had been a student of Socrates. He decided to follow his friend who was going to Persia to help the general Cyrus overthrow his brother, the king Artaxerxes. Xenophon went to Delphi upon the recommendation of Socrates but, having already made up his mind to go to Persia, consulted on a minor question only. He then set out for Asia Minor.

2. Describe the battle of Cunaxa.

   Cyrus' force was 110,000, including 10,000 Greeks. He marched from Sardis toward Susa and came up against the king's army of one million at Cunaxa. When the king's forces advanced, the Greeks led a counter charge and won the battle decisively. Cyrus was killed in an attack on Artaxerxes, and his troops fled.

3. What happened to the Greeks after the battle and why?

The Greeks were left alone against the king's huge army when the Persian army fled after the death of Cyrus. But, fearing them, the Persian general invited the Greek generals to a meeting, offering them guides and provisions for the return trip to Greece. Instead, the Persian general had the Greek generals slaughtered.

4. What did Xenophon do?

Xenophon encouraged his fearful soldiers to choose new leaders. He himself was chosen, among others. They decided on a retreat to the Black Sea, where they would be likely to find a friendly port and ships. The "ten thousand" spent five months in a retreat to the Black Sea.

5. Why did the Greeks consider this retreat a victory?

Confronting the Persians would have been suicide. The retreat, however, was successful and saved the army with few losses. It showed courage and ingenuity in dealing with obstacles and hardship, including terrible weather, lack of food, and unfriendly locals.

ACTIVITIES

1. Locate on Map 8:
   - Asia Minor
   - Sardis
   - Susa
   - Cunaxa
   - Babylon
   - Euxine (Black Sea)

2. Update the timeline of ancient Greece through the death of Socrates.

For the teacher:

Review the oracle at Delphi and the ceremony of consulting the priestess of the oracle with your students. Online, search: oracle delphi.

Delphi was on the slopes of Mt. Parnassus. The inner chamber of the shrine was built over a cleft in the rock.

A three-legged stool was over the cleft. The priestess took her seat on this stool. She would go into a trance and speak prophecy. The ancients believed that Apollo spoke through her, but it is now thought that she experienced the intoxicating effect of some kind of fume escaping from the rock. The prophecy was usually quite vague and open to interpretation.

LESSON 25: *Epaminondas and Pelopidas*
(Ἐπαμεινώνδας & Πελοπίδας)

FACTS TO KNOW

1. **Epaminondas** – Theban general and victor at Mantinea
2. **Pelopidas** – Theban hero at the battle of Leuctra
3. **Cadmea** – the citadel of Thebes

"Leuctra and Mantinea are daughters who will keep my name alive." – **Epaminondas**

"I have lived long enough." – **Epaminondas**

VOCABULARY

1. the **garrison** was taking a holiday _____ a permanent military post _____

COMPREHENSION QUESTIONS

1. Who were Epaminondas and Pelopidas? Describe how one saved the other in a battle.

   Epaminondas and Pelopidas were Thebans and close boyhood friends, although from opposite social classes. They went into the Theban army together and were fighting the Arcadians when Pelopidas was wounded. Epaminondas stayed with him and protected him until help arrived and took Pelopidas to safety.

2. How did Sparta take power in Thebes? What happened to Epaminondas and Pelopidas?

   A few wealthy Thebans betrayed their city to the Spartans in order to be made its rulers. On a day that the Cadmea was relatively undefended, these Thebans took a band of Spartan soldiers there. The Spartans held the citadel for four years. The rich Theban traitors became ruling tyrants. They banished some Theban soldiers, including Pelopidas. Not fearing the poor Epaminondas, they allowed him to stay, where he kept up training among the Theban youth.

3. How were the tyrants of Thebes overthrown?

Pelopidas went in exile to Athens, where he raised a force of other exiles and some Athenians. In the guise of a hunting party, his men made their way to Thebes. The tyrants were gathered at the home of a patriot who was in on the plot, where a few of Pelopidas' men, disguised as women, killed them. Pelopidas went into the houses of two other tyrants and killed them. The next morning the rest of Pelopidas' men came in, and the city rose up with them and retook the Cadmea.

4. What was the "sacred band" and what was the battle of Leuctra?

After eight years, Sparta tried to punish Thebes. The armies met at Leuctra. The Spartan force was twice as large as the Theban, but the Theban was much better drilled. Epaminondas was one of their leaders and won a great victory. Pelopidas led a force of 300 young men called "the sacred band," sworn to give their lives for the freedom of Thebes.

5. What circumstances led to the death of Pelopidas?

While helping the Thessalians gain their freedom from a tyrant ruler, Pelopidas was killed in a battle.

6. What was the battle of Mantinea?

Epaminondas led the Thebans against a combined force of Spartans and Athenians at Mantinea. The Thebans won a long, hard battle, but Epaminondas was wounded by a spear that could not be removed without killing him. Once he was sure of the victory, he removed the spear himself and died.

ACTIVITIES

1. Locate on Maps 2, 3:
   - Thebes
   - Leuctra
   - Mantinea
   - Arcadia
   - Thessaly

2. Update the timeline of ancient Greece with Leuctra and Mantinea.

REVIEW LESSON 5: *Lessons 21-25*

IMPORTANT DATES: *See Timeline*

776 B.C.	**1.**	First Olympic Games
401 B.C.	**2.**	battle of Cunaxa
371 B.C.	**3.**	battle of Leuctra
362 B.C.	**4.**	battle of Mantinea

IMPORTANT PEOPLE

Alcibiades	**1.**	Athenian naval commander who was exiled, then recalled
Nicias	**2.**	commander of the Athenian expedition to Sicily
Lysander	**3.**	Spartan admiral who captured Athens
Thrasybulus	**4.**	Athenian who overthrew the Tyrants
Socrates	**5.**	Athenian philosopher put to death for disrespecting the gods
Xanthippe	**6.**	wife of Socrates
Plato	**7.**	philosopher and pupil of Socrates
Xenophon	**8.**	Greek author of "The March Upcountry"
Artaxerxes	**9.**	the Persian king from whom the Greeks retreated
Epaminondas	**10.**	Theban general and victor at Mantinea
Pelopidas	**11.**	hero at the battle of Leuctra with his "sacred band"
Cyrus	**12.**	Persian general who attempted to seize his brother's throne

THINGS TO KNOW

Olympic Games	**1.**	important athletic contest of the Greeks, occurring every four years
Thirty Tyrants	**2.**	rulers installed at Athens by Sparta at end of Peloponnesian War
Academy	**3.**	school founded by Plato
Anabasis	**4.**	history of the retreat of the 10,000; "The March Upcountry"
Cadmea	**5.**	citadel of Thebes
Euxine	**6.**	Greek name for the Black Sea
Socratic method	**7.**	question-and-answer method of teaching

WHO SAID THAT?

1. "When the lion's skin is too short, you must patch it with that of a fox." _____ Lysander

2. "What! Would you have me die guilty?" _____ Socrates

3. "You can bury my body; you cannot put me into a grave." _____ Socrates

4. "I see the man." _____ Cyrus

5. "Leuctra and Mantinea are daughters who will keep my name alive." _____ Epaminondas

6. "I have lived long enough." _____ Epaminondas

7. "Thus died the man who was in death the noblest we have ever known, in life, the wisest and the best." _____ Plato

8. "And where can the good and the noble be found?" _____ Socrates

COMPREHENSION QUESTIONS TO REVIEW

1. Why was the expedition to Sicily undertaken, and what was its outcome?

    Alcibiades persuaded the Athenians to send an expedition to Syracuse because it was an ally of Sparta, because Athens needed its resources, and because it was assumed that it would be an easy target. It turned out to be the greatest disaster of the war for Athens, with a total loss of a very large and expensive fleet with all its men.

2. How was Lysander a fox at Ægos Potamos?

    Lysander lined up his ships as if ready to give battle, but when the Athenians approached, he did nothing. He repeated this performance for four days until the Athenians, assuming he was afraid, let their guard down. At this point, Lysander moved in and captured almost the entire Athenian fleet.

3. How was Socrates as much an example by his death as by his life?

    Socrates accepted his sentence gracefully and did not protest his innocence. He did not condemn his accusers or executioner. He used the month grace period he was given to commune with his friends and continue teaching. He taught that death is a passage to a nobler existence. He remained cheerful to the end.

4. Why did the Greeks consider the retreat of the 10,000 a victory?

Confronting the Persians would have been suicide. The retreat, however, was successful and saved the army with few losses. It showed courage and ingenuity in dealing with obstacles and hardship, including terrible weather, lack of food, and unfriendly locals.

5. How were the tyrants of Thebes overthrown?

Pelopidas went in exile to Athens, where he raised a force of other exiles and some Athenians. In the guise of a hunting party, his men made their way to Thebes. The tyrants were gathered at the home of a patriot who was in on the plot, where a few of Pelopidas' men, disguised as women, killed them. Pelopidas went into the houses of two remaining tyrants and killed them. The next morning, the rest of Pelopidas' men came in, and the city rose up with them and retook the Cadmea.

VOCABULARY

| hemlock | olympiad | garrison | fop | kinsman |
| cunning | philosophy | lot | plight | sentry |

__garrison__   1. a permanent military post

__olympiad__   2. four-year period between Olympic games

__fop__   3. dandy

__hemlock__   4. poison used for executions in ancient Greece

__kinsman__   5. relative

__plight__   6. difficulty; hardship

__sentry__   7. guard

__philosophy__   8. the love and pursuit of wisdom

__lot__   9. fortune; choice

__cunning__   10. showing artful deception or trickery

GEOGRAPHY REVIEW: *Study the location of the following places.*

Cities
- Aegos Potamos
- Leuctra
- Mantinea

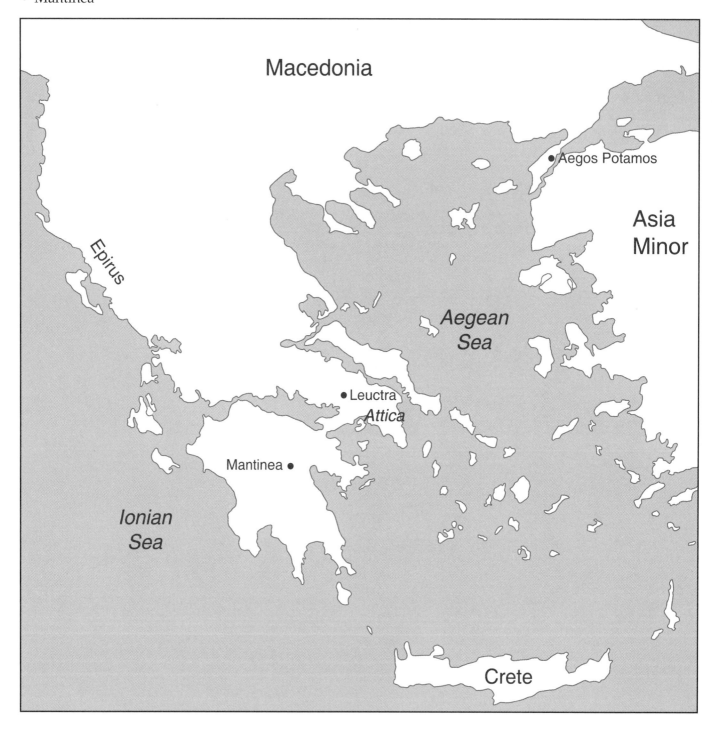

GEOGRAPHY REVIEW: *Use the following places to complete the maps.*

Cities

- Aegos Potamos
- Leuctra
- Mantinea

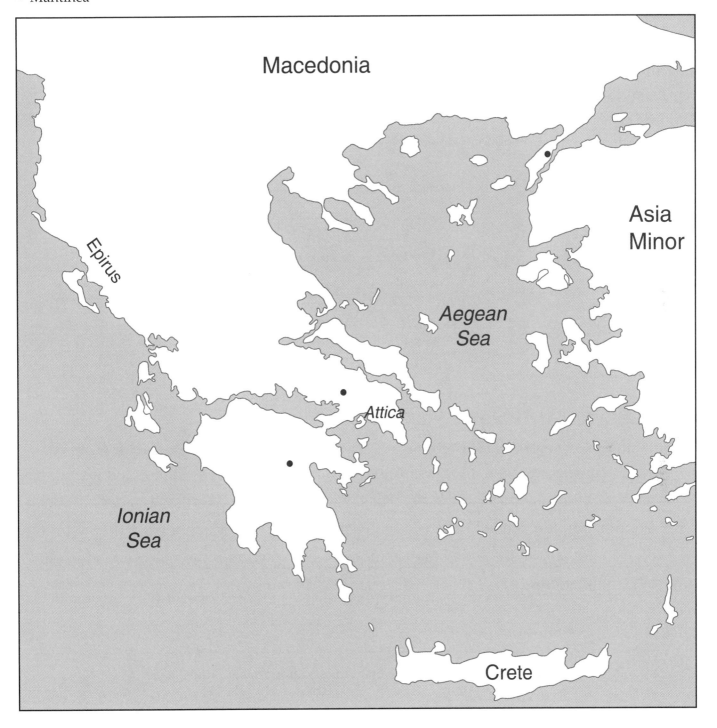

LESSON 26: *Philip (Φίλιππος) of Macedonia*

FACTS TO KNOW

1. **Macedonia** – state in northern Greece
2. **Philip II** – became king of Macedonia; father of Alexander
3. **Olympias** – wife of Philip
4. **phalanx** – close formation of infantry armed with long spears
5. **Demosthenes** – Athenian orator; warned against Philip

"I appeal from Philip drunk to Philip sober." – **Macedonian woman**

VOCABULARY

1. the **guardian** of the little king. _____ one who is legally responsible for a minor _____
2. **garlands** of vines and flowers. _____ wreaths _____
3. a **staff** twined with a vine branch. _____ stick; cane _____
4. **phalanx** (ancient meaning) _____ infantry formation (see above) _____
5. **phalanx** (modern meaning) _____ compact body of people _____

COMPREHENSION QUESTIONS

1. How did Philip become king of Macedonia, and how did the example of Thebes affect his ambition?

   The king was assassinated, his brother and heir was killed in battle, and his infant nephew succeeded to the throne. Philip was the infant's guardian but soon put him aside and made himself king. His ambition was to make Macedonia a great state after the example of the rise to greatness of Thebes under the military leadership of Epaminondas.

2. What military lesson did Philip learn from the Spartans and from Epaminondas?

   Philip knew that Sparta had become a great military power by requiring all of its young men to train as soldiers. He learned from Epaminondas to carefully drill his soldiers and how to arrange them in battle.

3. Give a general description of a phalanx. What were its strengths? (What was its weakness?)

A phalanx is a compact formation of infantry 16 rows deep. Each man holds in his right hand a 21-foot long spear forward and in his left a small round shield. The front row of men is preceded by the spear tips of the men in several rows back. A well-drilled phalanx was nearly impossible to defeat in a head-on attack. (It was, however, extremely vulnerable to attack from the rear, because it could not turn.)

4. How did Philip become master of Greece? What was the battle of Chæronea?

Aroused by the oratory of Demosthenes, Athens and Thebes joined forces to confront Philip. The armies met at Chæronea. The battle was a great victory for Philip and made him master of all Greece except Sparta.

5. What lessons in governing did Philip learn from the example of Sparta?

Philip learned not to rule as a tyrant. He acted generously toward conquered states, allowing each to manage their local affairs. General affairs were managed by a council.

ACTIVITIES

1. Locate on Maps 2, 3:
- Macedonia
- Epirus
- Chaeronea

For the teacher:
Have your students do some research on the phalanx formation. Describe, either verbally or in writing, what it would have felt like to be part of such a formation. Online, search: phalanx.

LESSON 27: *Alexander (Ἀλέξανδρος) the Great*

FACTS TO KNOW

1. **Alexander** – son of Philip; king of Macedonia; founder of a great empire from Greece to India
2. **Aristotle** – philosopher; teacher of Alexander
3. **Bucephalus** – Alexander's horse; "oxhead"
4. **Pindar** – Greek poet; wrote "The Odes"
5. **battle of the Granicus** – Alexander's first battle against the Persians
6. **Gordian knot** – slashed by Alexander; omen
7. **Darius III** – king of Persia
8. **battle of Issus** – Alexander's first defeat of Darius
9. **battle of Arbela** – Alexander's final defeat of Darius
10. **Roxana** – wife of Alexander
11. **Porus** – Indian king

"My father will leave me nothing to do!" – **Alexander**

"To the strongest." – **Alexander**

VOCABULARY

1. there were other **claimants** to the throne. persons who make a claim, such as to a throne
2. throwing off the Macedonian **yoke**. an oppressive power
3. The Thebans were **overawed** controlled or subdued by inspiring awe
4. The **scythes** went round with the wheels tools with long, curved blades
5. **scythe-chariot** chariot with blades extending from the wheel hubs
6. murdered by one of his own **satraps**. Persian provincial governors; officers
7. He drew his **signet ring** from his finger a ring with a seal

COMPREHENSION QUESTIONS

1. How did Alexander get his horse?

    Philip was offered a fine Thessalian horse that was so wild nobody could ride it.

    Alexander, still a boy, offered to ride it. He had noticed the horse was afraid of its own

    shadow, so he kept the horse facing into the sun and was able to ride him. He was

    given the horse, which became almost as famous as Alexander.

2. Briefly describe the key stages of Alexander's conquests.

a. battle at the Granicus: In the first move of his war against Persia, Alexander defeated the Persian general with a much smaller force. The Persian general killed himself. Sardis was taken without opposition.

b. Gordium: At Gordium in Phrygia, Alexander showed his boldness and ability to get to the heart of the matter by slicing the famous Gordian knot. Little resistance followed across Asia Minor.

c. battle of Issus: Alexander's first battle against Darius in person. Darius was badly beaten and fled, leaving his mother, wife, and children, who were treated kindly and respectfully by Alexander.

d. Damascus and the siege of Tyre: Alexander took Damascus and then lay siege to Tyre, which lasted seven months. Alexander sold thousands of Tyrians into slavery.

e. Jerusalem and Egypt: Jerusalem and Egypt were taken without a battle. The people were tired of Persian rule.

f. Alexandria: Alexander founded his namesake city on the Nile delta. He made Jews welcome. Alexandria was for a long time the center of culture and learning of the ancient world.

g. battle of Arbela: Alexander's final battle with Darius, who had an army of 1,000,000 with scythe-chariots and elephants. Darius was beaten and fled.

h. Babylon, Susa, and Persepolis: Babylon and Susa submitted without resistance. Persepolis, with its huge treasure, was taken.

i. Bactria: Alexander conquered Bactria and married the princess Roxana.

j. battle at the Hydaspes: Turning his sights on India, Alexander went through the Kyber Pass and defeated King Porus at the Hydaspes. At this point, Alexander turned back.

3. Describe Alexander's death and the disposition of his empire.

Alexander died at age 32 of a fever. His last instructions were to make the strongest of his generals his successor. (In fact, his empire was divided among his top generals and rapidly disintegrated.)

ACTIVITIES

1. Locate on Map 9:
   - Ephesus
   - Granicus River
   - Sardis
   - Phrygia
   - Gordium
   - Issus
   - Damascus
   - Tyre
   - Syria
   - Egypt
   - Jerusalem
   - Alexandria
   - Arbela
   - Persia
   - Babylon
   - Susa
   - Persepolis
   - Bactria
   - India
   - Khaiber (Kyber) Pass
   - Hydaspes River
   - Indus River

LESSON 28: *Demosthenes (Δημοσθένης)*

FACTS TO KNOW

1. **Demosthenes** – Athenian orator; warned against Philip in his most famous series of speeches, the Philippics
2. **Philippics** – Demosthenes' speeches against Philip of Macedonia

"Do not be discouraged but conquer your difficulties." – **actor to Demosthenes**

"Let us be equally energetic and unselfish and just, then we shall triumph." – **Demosthenes**

"I insist that even if it had been known beforehand to all the world that Philip would succeed and that we should fail, not even then ought Athens to have taken any other course if she had any regard for her own glory or for her past or for the ages to come." – **Demosthenes**

VOCABULARY

1. **philippic** _____tirade; harsh verbal denunciation_____
2. the end of his writing **quill**. _____shaft of a feather, prepared for use as a writing instrument_____
3. who taught **declamation**. _____speaking loudly with persuasive effect_____
4. the orator was absolutely **incorruptible** _____incapable of being morally corrupted_____

COMPREHENSION QUESTIONS

1. What first motivated Demosthenes to become a lawyer?

   Demosthenes was robbed of his inheritance by his guardians. When he heard an important case being argued by a famous lawyer, who won his case, he decided that this was the way to get his inheritance back.

2. How did Demosthenes overcome his difficulties with speech and body language?

   To overcome stammering, he practiced speaking with stones in his mouth. To accustom himself to the noise of the public assembly, he practiced speaking at the beach over the roar of the ocean. To correct a habit of lifting one shoulder, he spoke with a sword suspended over the other shoulder. He isolated himself for months practicing. To learn oratory, he studied with the speaker Isæus.

3. Why did Demosthenes oppose Philip, and what did he point to as the main source of weakness among the Greeks?

Demosthenes saw Philip as a threat to Athenian and Greek liberty. He saw the Greeks as complacent and lacking energy.

4. How did Philip try to silence Demosthenes? How did Alexander try, and what happened?

Philip tried to bribe Demosthenes. Alexander tried to have him handed over to be tried for treason. Demosthenes persuaded the Athenians that it would be their necks next, and they protected him.

5. How did Demosthenes die?

After Alexander's death, Macedonia again demanded Demosthenes be handed over. He took refuge in a temple, which was surrounded by soldiers promising him pardon if he gave himself up. Not trusting this, he asked for time to write a letter, and poisoned himself with a quill he had prepared for such an eventuality.

ACTIVITIES

1. Update the timeline of ancient Greece through the death of Alexander.

For the teacher:
Have your students find and read one of the Philippics of Demosthenes. Have them report on the speech, the nature of the argument, and the style of the denunciation.

LESSON 29: *Aristotle (Ἀριστοτέλης), Zeno, Diogenes, and Apelles*

FACTS TO KNOW

1. **Aristotle** – philosopher; teacher of Alexander
2. **Zeno** – philosopher; Stoic school of philosophy
3. **Epicurus** – philosopher; Epicurean school of philosophy
4. **Diogenes** – philosopher; Cynic school of philosophy
5. **Apelles** – painter

"Sell me to someone who wishes a master." – **Diogenes**

"Never a day without a line." – **Apelles**

"I am looking for a man." – **Diogenes**

"If I were not going to conquer the world, I should like to have the power which Diogenes has to conquer self." – **Alexander the Great**

VOCABULARY

1. **stoic** (modern meaning) ___ indifferent to pleasure or pain ___
2. **epicurean** (modern meaning) ___ devoted to good food and drink ___
3. **cynic** (modern meaning) ___ one who believes all people are motivated by selfishness ___

COMPREHENSION QUESTIONS

1. Why did Aristotle make enemies, and why did he flee Athens?
   Aristotle made enemies because his teachings, based on logic and reason, were considered by certain elements of the citizenry to be against religion. He claimed to have fled Athens to prevent these people from attacking philosophy itself by banishing him.

2. How did the Stoics get their name, and what is the essence of the Stoic philosophy?
   The name "Stoic" comes from Stoa, a name for a kind of open-air gallery, where Zeno gave his lectures. The essence of Stoic philosophy is that the world is as it was meant to be and that men should be virtuous and accept whatever comes without complaint.

3. What is the essence of the Epicurean philosophy, and what is the common misconception about it?

The essence of Epicurean philosophy is that pleasure is the highest good and should be the goal of men. "Pleasure" meant pursuit of knowledge, peace of mind, and avoidance of pain. It was and is often mistakenly taken to mean the pursuit of pleasure through eating, drinking, and living for the day.

4. Why is it likely that Diogenes did not have many friends among the citizenry of Athens? Can you guess why Alexander might have liked him for the same reason?

Diogenes was apparently quite eccentric and publicly ridiculed his fellow citizens, which won him an audience, but probably few friends. Alexander might have found Diogenes' rough and blunt speech refreshing, as there were few people who would dare to contradict him or speak back to him.

5. What is the story of Apelles and the horses? As this story is unlikely to be fact, what idea do you suppose it is used to convey?

Apelles is said to have exhibited a painting of a horse, along with other painters who had also painted horses. Although the judges rejected Apelles' painting, real horses preferred it to the others. This implies that a person should have the self-confidence to place his own standards above that of prize judges.

ACTIVITIES

1. Locate on Maps 1, 2:
   - Athens
   - Corinth
   - Crete

For the teacher:
Have your students do some extra research on the schools of Epicureanism, Stoicism, and Cynicism. Online, search: Epicureanism, Stoicism, Cynicism, Greek philosophy.

LESSON 30: *Ptolemy (Πτολεμαῖος)*

FACTS TO KNOW

1. **Ptolemy** – one of Alexander's generals; assumed rule of Egypt in the division of Alexander's empire
2. **Ptolemy Philadelphus** – son of Ptolemy; built Alexandrian library; had Hebrew Bible translated into Greek; reopened the Red Sea canal
3. **Cleopatra** – last monarch of the Ptolemy line

VOCABULARY

1. **pith** of the papyrus ____soft, spongy center of plant stems____
2. pith of the **papyrus** ____tall, aquatic plant used to make a paper-like writing medium____
3. the earth's **circumference**____boundary line of a circle or sphere____
4. the earth's ... **diameter**.____straight line passing from opposite edges through the center of a____ circle or sphere

COMPREHENSION QUESTIONS

1. What happened to Alexander's empire after his death?

   After Alexander's death, his empire was divided among four of his generals. Ptolemy became the Greek pharaoh of Egypt. The other three generals became first regents, then kings of their respective portions of the empire.

2. Which city in Egypt was founded by Alexander, and what did Ptolemy do with it?

   Alexander founded Alexandria. Ptolemy made it his capital, brought Alexander's body there, and placed it in a mausoleum. He began collecting works for the great library.

3. Who was Ptolemy's son, and what were his beneficial policies and acts?

   Ptolemy's son, Ptolemy Philadelphus, continued to build the library. He made Alexandria a welcome place for Jews and made use of their skills and learning. He commissioned the translation of the Hebrew Bible into Greek and cleared the ancient canal linking the Nile to the Red Sea.

4. What became of Alexander's city?

Alexandria became a great center of commerce and learning. The library and associated schools became the best in the world, where the best philosophers and scientists came to teach and do research. (It was the second largest city of the Roman Empire, after Rome itself, and is an important port of Egypt today.)

5. What became of the Ptolemy line?

The Ptolemy line ruled Egypt for over 350 years, into the Roman period. The last monarch of the line was Cleopatra. (After her death, Augustus made Egypt a province of the Roman Empire.)

ACTIVITIES

1. Locate on Map 5:
   - Memphis
   - Alexandria
   - Red Sea
   - Nile River
   - Nile Delta
   - ancient Red Sea canal
   - Suez Canal

> *For the teacher:*
> Have your students investigate how papyrus was made and report on what they find out. For example, what kind of plant is papyrus? How is it prepared? What is the process of making it into a writing material? Online, search: papyrus.

REVIEW LESSON 6: *Lessons 26-30*

IMPORTANT DATES: *See Timeline.*

336 B.C.	**1.**	death of Philip; Alexander becomes king of Macedonia
323 B.C.	**2.**	death of Alexander

IMPORTANT PEOPLE

Philip II	**1.**	king of Macedonia; father of Alexander the Great
Olympias	**2.**	his wife
Demosthenes	**3.**	Athenian orator who warned against growing Macedonian power
Alexander	**4.**	founder of the greatest empire of the pre-Roman world
Aristotle	**5.**	philosopher and teacher of Alexander
Roxana	**6.**	wife of Alexander
Bucephalus	**7.**	Alexander's horse
Darius III	**8.**	king of Persia defeated by Alexander
Porus	**9.**	last monarch defeated by Alexander
Ptolemy	**10.**	general who ruled Egypt after Alexander's death
Ptolemy Philadelphus	**11.**	ruler who made Alexandria a center of learning
Cleopatra	**12.**	last of the Ptolemies
Zeno	**13.**	founder of Stoic school of philosophy
Epicurus	**14.**	founder of Epicurean school of philosophy
Diogenes	**15.**	founder of the Cynics
Pindar	**16.**	poet; author of "The Odes"

THINGS TO KNOW

Gordian knot	**1.**	complicated knot "untied" by Alexander
battle of the Granicus	**2.**	Alexander's first battle against the Persians
battle of Arbela	**3.**	Alexander's last defeat of Darius III
Philippics	**4.**	series of speeches by Demosthenes against Philip
Ptolemies	**5.**	Egyptian monarchs descended from one of Alexander's generals
Alexandria	**6.**	city founded by and named after Alexander the Great
Stoics	**7.**	school of philosophy that teaches simple living

Epicureans _____ 8. school of philosophy that teaches the pursuit of peace of mind

Cynics _____ 9. philosophy that assumes all men are motivated by selfishness

WHO SAID THAT?

1. "I appeal from Philip drunk to Philip sober." _____ Macedonian woman

2. "My father will leave me nothing to do!" _____ Alexander

3. "To the strongest." _____ Alexander

4. "Let us be equally energetic and unselfish and just, then we shall triumph." _____ Demosthenes

5. "Sell me to someone who wishes a master." _____ Diogenes

6. "Never a day without a line." _____ Apelles

7. "If I were not going to conquer the world, I should like to have the power which Diogenes has to conquer self." _____ Alexander

8. "Do not be discouraged but conquer your difficulties." _____ actor to Demosthenes

COMPREHENSION QUESTIONS TO REVIEW

1. What military lessons and lessons in governing did Philip learn from the Spartans?

Philip knew that Sparta had become a great military power by requiring all of its young men to train as soldiers. He learned from Epaminondas to carefully drill his soldiers and how to arrange them in battle.

Philip learned not to rule as a tyrant. He acted generously toward conquered states, allowing each to manage their local affairs. General affairs were managed by a council.

2. List, in order, the key stages of Alexander's conquests.
   a. battle of the Granicus
   b. Gordium
   c. battle of Issus
   d. Damascus and the siege of Tyre
   e. Jerusalem and Egypt
   f. Alexandria
   g. battle of Arbela
   h. Babylon, Susa, and Persepolis
   i. Bactria
   j. battle of Hydaspes

3. How did Demosthenes overcome his difficulties as a public speaker?

To overcome stammering, he practiced speaking with stones in his mouth. To accustom himself to the noise of the public assembly, he practiced speaking at the beach over the roar of the ocean. To correct a habit of lifting one shoulder, he spoke with a sword suspended over the other shoulder. He isolated himself for months practicing. To learn oratory, he studied with the speaker Isæus.

4. Briefly describe the Stoic and Epicurean philosophies in the ancient context.

The essence of Stoic philosophy is that the world is as it was meant to be and that men should be virtuous and accept whatever comes without complaint. The essence of Epicurean philosophy is that pleasure is the highest good and should be the goal of men. "Pleasure" meant pursuit of knowledge, peace of mind, and avoidance of pain. It was and is often mistakenly taken to mean the pursuit of pleasure through eating, drinking, and living for the day.

5. What became of Alexandria, and what became of the Ptolemies?

Alexandria became a great center of commerce and learning. The library and associated schools became the best in the world, where the best philosophers and scientists came to teach and do research. The Ptolemy line ruled Egypt for over 350 years, into the Roman period. The last monarch of the line was Cleopatra.

VOCABULARY

satrap	diameter	papyrus	pith	scythe	epicurean
circumference	declamation	signet ring	claimant	stoic	guardian
cynic	phalanx	philippic	quill	garland	
scythe-chariot	overawe	incorruptible	staff	yoke	

circumference	**1.**	boundary line of a circle or sphere
quill	**2.**	shaft of a feather prepared for use as a writing instrument
scythe	**3.**	tool with a long, curved blade
staff	**4.**	stick or cane
pith	**5.**	soft, spongy center of plant stems
stoic	**6.**	indifferent to pain or pleasure
claimant	**7.**	one who makes a claim, such as to a throne
phalanx	**8.**	compact body of people
guardian	**9.**	one legally responsible for a minor
satrap	**10.**	Persian provincial governor
yoke	**11.**	an oppressive power
cynic	**12.**	one who believes all people are motivated by selfishness
papyrus	**13.**	aquatic plant used to make paper
overawe	**14.**	to subdue by inspiring awe
garland	**15.**	wreath
scythe-chariot	**16.**	chariot with blades on the hubs
diameter	**17.**	a straight line passing from opposite edges through the center of a circle or sphere
epicurean	**18.**	devoted to good food and drink
signet ring	**19.**	a ring with a seal
phalanx	**20.**	Greek infantry formation
philippic	**21.**	harsh verbal denunciation
declamation	**22.**	speaking loudly with persuasive effect
incorruptible	**23.**	incapable of being morally corrupted

GEOGRAPHY REVIEW: *Study the location of the following places.*

Countries, Islands
- **Macedonia**
- Bactria
- **India**
- Syria
- **Egypt**
- **Persia**

Cities
- **Gordium**
- **Babylon**
- Issus
- Damascus
- Jerusalem
- **Alexandria**
- Arbela
- Persepolis

Bodies of Water, Mountains
- Granicus River
- Hydaspes River

For the teacher:
The terms in bold are required for memorization.
The unbolded terms can be used for bonus.

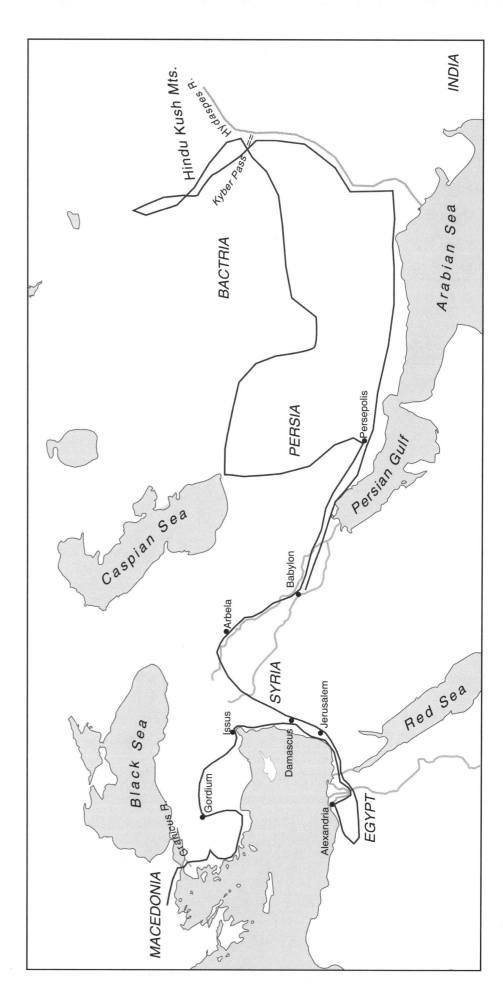

GEOGRAPHY REVIEW: *Use the following places to complete the maps.*

Countries, Islands

- **Macedonia**
- Bactria
- **India**
- Syria
- **Egypt**
- **Persia**

Cities

- **Gordium**
- **Babylon**
- Issus
- Damascus
- Jerusalem
- **Alexandria**
- Arbela
- Persepolis

Bodies of Water, Mountains

- Granicus River
- Hydaspes River

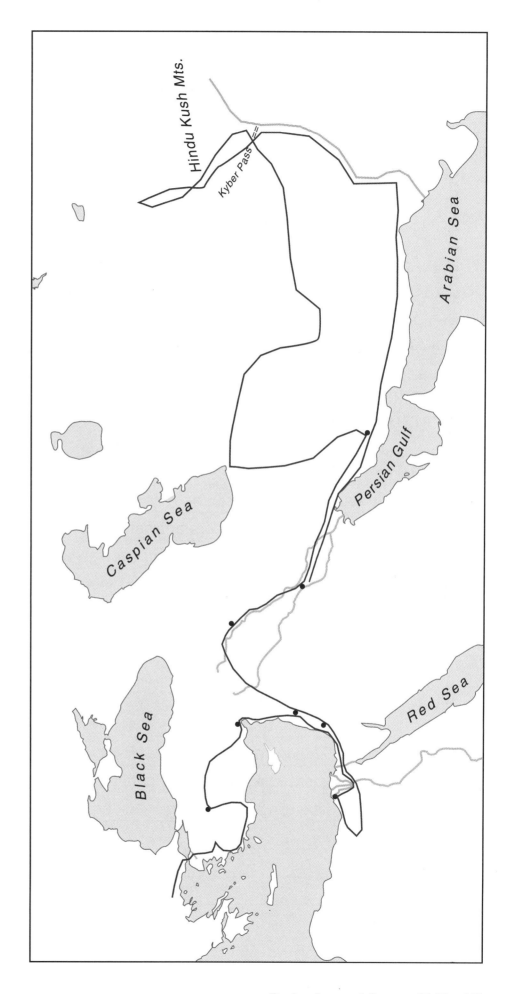

LESSON 31: *Pyrrhus (Πύρρος)*

FACTS TO KNOW

1. **Pyrrhus** – king of Epirus who won costly victories against the Romans
2. **Archimedes** – mathematician and engineer of Syracuse

"Another such victory and I shall have to go home alone." – **Pyrrhus**

VOCABULARY

1. **pyrrhic victory** _____ victory won with unacceptable losses
2. to poison his master for the **consuls**. _____ highest magistrates of the Roman Republic
3. his good fortune **forsook** [forsake] him. to abandon; to give up; to renounce

COMPREHENSION QUESTIONS

1. Outline the reasons Pyrrhus was not known as a lover of peace.

   Not content with the kingdom he inherited, Pyrrhus attacked Macedonia. He eagerly
   came to the aid of Greeks in southern Italy in a war against the Romans. He went to
   Sicily to fight with the Greeks there against the Carthaginians and fought a second
   war in southern Italy. He fought a second war against Macedonia, invaded the
   Peloponnesus, and took part in a civil war in Argos.

2. Describe the battle that gives us the term "pyrrhic victory."

   Pyrrhus came at the request of Greeks in southern Italy against the Romans. He
   came with 30,000 men and 20 elephants. Pyrrhus won a victory, but with the loss of
   half his men. His losses were so great that the victory was as bad as, or worse than, a
   defeat. This is the origin and meaning of the term "pyrrhic victory."

3. How did Pyrrhus' second battle in southern Italy come to an end?

A servant of Pyrrhus went to the Romans, offering to poison his master for them. The Romans scorned such a way of winning and sent the servant back to Pyrrhus. In gratitude, Pyrrhus returned all his Roman prisoners without ransom and made a truce, under the terms of which he agreed to leave Italy.

4. How did Pyrrhus break his agreement with the Romans, and what did it cost him?

While in Sicily, Pyrrhus received a call for aid from the same Greeks in southern Italy for whom he had fought before. Against the terms of his truce with the Romans, he reentered southern Italy, was defeated, and forced out of Italy for good.

5. Who was Archimedes, and how did he die?

Archimedes was an engineer and mathematician of Greek Syracuse. He invented many devices, including a range of war machines. During the Roman siege of Syracuse, he was killed by a Roman soldier who had no idea who he was.

ACTIVITIES

1. Locate on Maps 2-4:
   - Epirus
   - Macedonia
   - Adriatic Sea
   - Great Greece (Magna Graecia)
   - Sicily
   - Syracuse
   - Carthage
   - Peloponnesus
   - Argos

> *For the teacher:*
> Have your students research and report on some of the inventions of Archimedes. Online, search: Archimedes.

LESSON 32: *Cleomenes III (Κλεομένης)*

FACTS TO KNOW

1. **Cleomenes III** – king of Sparta who tried to restore the laws of Lycurgus

2. **Leonidas** – joint king of Sparta; father of Cleomenes

3. **Agis** – joint king of Sparta with Leonidas; murdered by Leonidas

4. **Agiatis** – widow of Agis; wife of Cleomenes

5. **Aratus** – general of the Achæan League

6. **Achæan League** – league of Greek city-states

7. **Antigonus** – Macedonian king who defeated Sparta

> *"If without bloodshed I could have driven from Sparta luxury and extravagance, debts and usury, the riches of the few and the poverty of the many, I should have thought myself the happiest of kings."* – **Cleomenes III**

VOCABULARY

1. the five **ephors** of Sparta_____ magistrates of Sparta_____

2. **tread** in the steps of Lycurgus ___ to walk; to step_____

COMPREHENSION QUESTIONS

1. Why was Cleomenes recalled to the palace?

   Cleomenes' father, Leonidas, recalled him to the palace to be married that very evening to the widow of Agis.

2. Why was Cleomenes surprised at his father's arrangement, and what came of it?

   Cleomenes was surprised because his father had murdered his co-king Agis, husband of the prospective bride Agiatis. Although Agiatis hated Leonidas, she came to love Cleomenes and shared his goals for Sparta.

3. What had changed in Sparta since Lycurgus? What did Cleomenes want to do, who opposed him, and what did he do about it?

The citizenry of Sparta had gone from disciplined and well-trained to a lifestyle of luxury and selfishness. Cleomenes committed himself to restoring the laws and disciplines of Lycurgus and Solon. He was opposed by the ephors and many of the citizens. He had the ephors killed, and banished 80 citizens.

4. What put an end to Spartan independence?

Sparta was defeated in a single battle by the Achæan League, with the assistance of King Antigonus of Macedonia.

5. What did Cleomenes try to do, and what was the outcome?

Cleomenes sought aid from Ptolemy, but Ptolemy died. Cleomenes was then accused of plotting against the Egyptian king and imprisoned. Seeing no escape, he took his own life.

ACTIVITIES

1. Update the timeline of ancient Greece through the defeat of Sparta by the Achæan League.

LESSON 33: *The Fall of Greece*

FACTS TO KNOW

1. **Perseus** – Macedonian king defeated by Romans

VOCABULARY

1. she **revolted** [**revolt**] from Turkey _____ to rebel; to attempt to overthrow _____

2. light of art and science that she **kindled** [**kindle**] _____ to ignite; to spark _____

COMPREHENSION QUESTIONS

1. How did Greek independence end?

   The Greek city-states failed to throw off Macedonian rule, which continued for a

   century. Macedonia and Epirus were conquered by the Romans, followed by the rest

   of Greece, which became part of the Roman Empire. This was due in large part to

   Greek city-states fighting amongst themselves and not showing a united front against

   their enemies.

2. List some of the accomplishments of the ancient Greeks and the words that have entered our language

   relating to these accomplishments.

   • science of numbers: arithmetic, mathematics

   • high development of sports in ancient Greece: gymnasium, athletics

   • highest literary art form of the ancient Greeks: poet, poetry, poem

   • the theories and practice of language and argument: grammar, rhetoric

   • study of the world, its lands, and peoples was advanced by the Greeks: geography

   • the science of clear, provable thought: logic

   • the study of the night sky: astronomy

   • medical science and practice was advanced by the Greeks: surgery

ACTIVITIES

1. Update the timeline through the Roman defeat and loss of Greek independence.

> *For the teacher:*
> Have your students, either individually or as a group, tell the story of Greece from its mythic beginnings to its defeat by the Romans. Summarize the contributions of the Greeks to our own culture. As an individual activity, this can be done as a report. As a group activity, it can be done as a series of recitations, or even as a kind of play.

REVIEW LESSON 7: *Lessons 31-33*

IMPORTANT DATES: *See Timeline.*

279 B.C.	1.	Pyrrhus wins "pyrrhic victory" over the Romans
222 B.C.	2.	defeat of Sparta by the Achæan League
220-196 B.C.	3.	first Roman victories in Greece
146 B.C.	4.	Greece becomes a Roman province

IMPORTANT PEOPLE

Pyrrhus	1.	king of Epirus who won costly victories against the Romans
Archimedes	2.	mathematician and engineer of Syracuse
Cleomenes III	3.	king of Sparta who tried to restore the laws of Lycurgus
Antigonus	4.	Macedonian king who defeated Sparta
Aratus	5.	general of the Achæan League
Agis	6.	joint king of Sparta; murdered by Leonidas
Leonidas	7.	joint king of Sparta; father of Cleomenes
Perseus	8.	Macedonian king defeated by Romans

THINGS TO KNOW

Achæan League	1.	league of Greek city-states that defeated Sparta

WHO SAID THAT?

1. "Another such victory and I shall have to go home alone." Pyrrhus

2. "If without bloodshed I could have driven from Sparta luxury and extravagance, debts and usury, the riches of the few and the poverty of the many, I should have thought myself the happiest of kings."
    Cleomenes III

COMPREHENSION QUESTIONS TO REVIEW

1. Who was Archimedes, and how did he die?
    Archimedes was an engineer and mathematician of Greek Syracuse. He invented many devices, including a range of war machines. During the Roman siege of Syracuse, he was killed by a Roman soldier who had no idea who he was.

2. What had changed in Sparta, and what did Cleomenes III try to do about it?

The citizenry of Sparta had gone from disciplined and well-trained to a lifestyle of luxury and selfishness. Cleomenes committed himself to restoring the laws and disciplines of Lycurgus and Solon. He was opposed by the ephors and many of the citizens. He had the ephors killed, and banished 80 citizens.

3. How did Greek independence end?

The Greek city-states failed to throw off Macedonian rule, which continued for a century. Macedonia and Epirus were conquered by the Romans, followed by the rest of Greece, which became part of the Roman Empire. This was due in large part to Greek city-states fighting amongst themselves and not showing a united front against their enemies.

4. Who do you believe is the greatest Greek hero and why?

Answers will vary.

NOTE: *Study the Greek History Timeline*

VOCABULARY

ephor	revolt	consul	kindle	forsake	tread	pyrrhic victory

tread	**1.**	to walk over
consul	**2.**	one of two ruling magistrates of the Roman Republic
ephor	**3.**	magistrate of Sparta
pyrrhic victory	**4.**	victory not worth the cost
forsake	**5.**	to abandon or renounce
revolt	**6.**	to rebel; to attempt to overthrow
kindle	**7.**	to ignite; to spark

GEOGRAPHY REVIEW: *Study the location of the following places.*

Countries, Islands
- Macedonia
- Sicily
- Magna Graecia

Cities
- Carthage
- Syracuse
- Argos

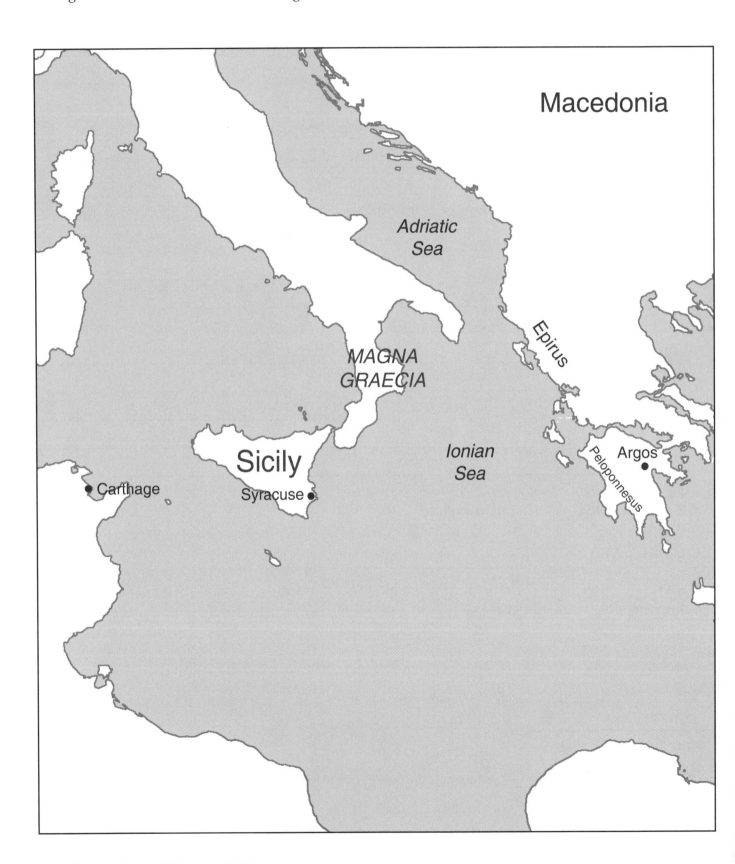

GEOGRAPHY REVIEW: *Use the following places to complete the maps.*

Countries, Islands
- Macedonia
- Sicily
- Magna Graecia

Cities
- Carthage
- Syracuse
- Argos

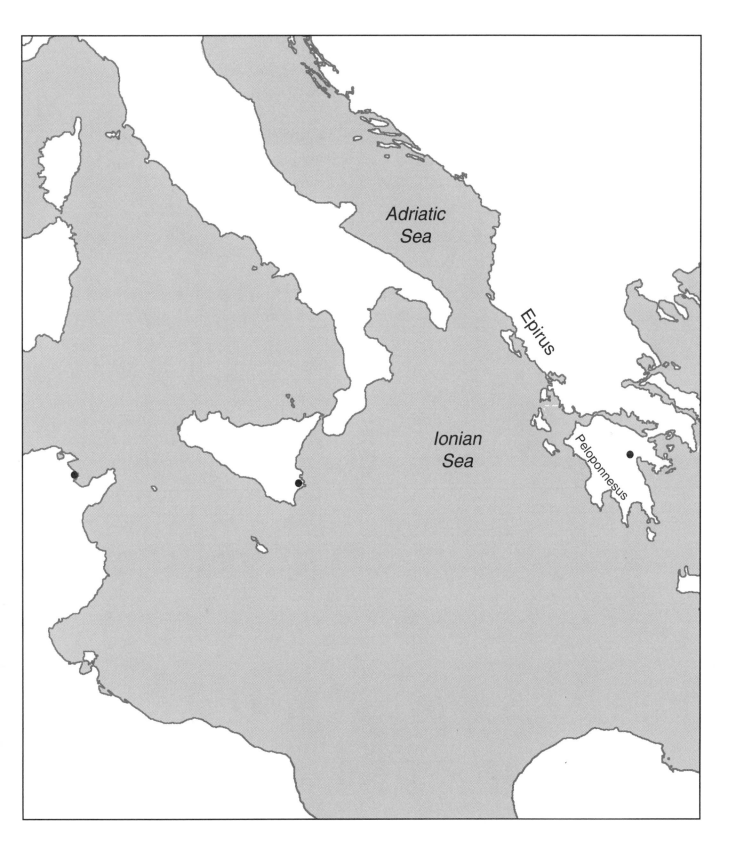

GREEK GODS AND THEIR ROMAN NAMES

Famous Men of Greece usually refers to the Greek gods by their Roman names. As this is a story about Greece, however, this study guide uses the Greek names of the gods and encourages the student to become as familiar with them as they already are with the Roman names. The only exception is our use of the Roman name Hercules.

To keep the names straight, copy this table and keep it handy as a reference.

Greek name	Roman name
Zeus	Jupiter (Juppiter)
Hera	Juno
Poseidon	Neptune
Hades	Pluto
Demeter	Ceres
Hestia	Vesta
Kerberus	Cerberus
Persephone	Proserpine
Hermes	Mercury
Hephaestus	Vulcan
Ares	Mars
Apollo	Apollo
Artemis	Diana
Athena	Minerva
Aphrodite	Venus
Eros	Cupid
Herakles	Hercules

WHO SAID THAT? WORKSHEET

1. Cast behind you the bones of your mother.	Parnassus oracle
2. Building is better than killing.	Cadmus
3. See! I have brought you that which you desired.	Perseus
4. What had been fated came to pass.	Greek saying
5. I will get you some of the apples if you will hold up the sky for me.	Atlas
6. Beware of the man who wears but one sandal.	oracle of Apollo
7. If you are a man, lift that stone.	Æthra
8. If my death will help the Greeks, I am ready to die.	Iphigenia
9. I care nothing for gods! But as for men, let me show you how much I like them!	Cyclops
10. Loose me! Loose me! I must go nearer that music!	Odysseus
11. Bring up this child for Sparta.	order of Sparta
12. Come back with this or upon this.	Spartan mothers
13. Sparta's citizens are her walls.	Lycurgus
14. Who is the happiest man you have ever known?	Crœsus
15. I call no man happy until he is dead. When I hear whether or not your life has ended nobly, then I shall know whether or not you were really happy.	Solon
16. Men of Athens! See what my enemies have done to me because I am a friend of the people.	Pisistratus
17. There you will find both earth and water for your master.	the Spartans
18. Rejoice! Rejoice! We are victors!	Phidippides
19. So much the better, we shall fight in the shade.	Spartan soldier
20. Stranger, tell the Spartans that we lie here in obedience to their commands.	Spartan memorial
21. We fight for all.	Greeks at Salamis
22. I have never seen him but I am tired of hearing him called "the Just."	Athenian to Aristides
23. Athens and Sparta are the two legs of Greece.	Cimon
24. Because Cimon is already with me.	oracle of Zeus

25. That of which I am proudest is that no Athenian ever wore mourning because of anything done by me.	Pericles
26. What you praise in my life has been due to fortune. I deserve no credit for it.	Pericles
27. When the lion's skin is too short, you must patch it with that of a fox.	Lysander
28. What! Would you have me die guilty?	Socrates
29. You can bury my body; you cannot put me into a grave.	Socrates
30. My judges, you go now to your homes, I to prison and to death. But which of the two is the better lot, God only knows.	Socrates
31. Thus died the man who was in death the noblest we have ever known, in life, the wisest and the best.	Plato
32. Victory!	Greeks at Cunaxa
33. I see the man.	Cyrus
34. And where can the good and the noble be found?	Socrates
35. Leuctra and Mantinea are daughters who will keep my name alive.	Epaminondas
36. I have lived long enough.	Epaminondas
37. I appeal from Philip drunk to Philip sober.	Macedonian woman
38. My father will leave me nothing to do!	Alexander
39. To the strongest.	Alexander
40. Do not be discouraged but conquer your difficulties.	actor to Demosthenes
41. Let us be equally energetic and unselfish and just, then we shall triumph.	Demosthenes
42. I insist that even if it had been known beforehand to all the world that Philip would succeed and that we should fail, not even then ought Athens to have taken any other course if she had any regard for her own glory or for her past or for the ages to come.	Demosthenes
43. Sell me to someone who wishes a master.	Diogenes
44. Never a day without a line.	Apelles
45. I am looking for a man.	Diogenes
46. If I were not going to conquer the world, I should like to have the power which Diogenes has to conquer self.	Alexander
47. Another such victory and I shall have to go home alone.	Pyrrhus
48. If without bloodshed I could have driven from Sparta luxury and extravagance, debts and usury, the riches of the few and the poverty of the many, I should have thought myself the happiest of kings.	Cleomenes III

GREEK HISTORY TIMELINE WORKSHEET

DATE	EVENT	DESCRIPTION
c. 1200 B.C.	Trojan War	Trojans defeated by the Greeks
825 B.C.	Lycurgus	reformed laws in Sparta
776 B.C.	first Olympic games	held in Elis
624 B.C.	Draco's code	reformed laws in Athens
c. 594 B.C.	Solon's reforms	further reformed laws in Athens
c. 560 B.C.	coup of Pisistratus	seized the Acropolis in Athens
527 B.C.	death of Pisistratus	
490 B.C.	battle of Marathon	Greeks defeat Persians; Darius I
480 B.C.	battles of Thermopylæ, Salamis	Greeks defeat Persians; Xerxes
479 B.C.	battle of Platæa	final battle against Persians
468 B.C.	Cimon defeats Persians	pursued Persians on land and sea
443-429 B.C.	Pericles dominates Athenian politics	
431-404 B.C.	Peloponnesian War	civil war between Sparta and Athens
430 B.C.	plague at Athens	
401 B.C.	battle of Cunaxa	Greeks aid Cyrus against Artaxerxes
399 B.C.	trial and death of Socrates	
371 B.C.	battle of Leuctra	Thebes defeats Sparta
362 B.C.	battle of Mantinea	Thebes defeats Sparta and Athens
336 B.C.	death of Philip	Alexander becomes king
323 B.C.	death of Alexander	Ptolemy rules Egypt
279 B.C.	Pyrrhus defeats Romans at Asculum	pyrrhic victory
222 B.C.	defeat of Sparta by Achæan League	
220-196 B.C.	first Roman victories in Greece	
146 B.C.	Greece becomes a Roman province	

GREEK HISTORY TIMELINE WORKSHEET

DATE	EVENT	DESCRIPTION
c. 1200 B.C.	Trojan War	Trojans defeated by the Greeks
825 B.C.	Lycurgus	reformed laws in Sparta
776 B.C.	first Olympic games	held in Elis
624 B.C.	Draco's code	reformed laws in Athens
c. 594 B.C.	Solon's reforms	further reformed laws in Athens
c. 560 B.C.	coup of Pisistratus	seized the Acropolis in Athens
527 B.C.	death of Pisistratus	
490 B.C.	battle of Marathon	Greeks defeat Persians; Darius I
480 B.C.	battles of Thermopylæ, Salamis	Greeks defeat Persians; Xerxes
479 B.C.	battle of Platæa	final battle against Persians
468 B.C.	Cimon defeats Persians	pursued Persians on land and sea
443-429 B.C.	Pericles dominates Athenian politics	
431-404 B.C.	Peloponnesian War	civil war between Sparta and Athens
430 B.C.	plague at Athens	
401 B.C.	battle of Cunaxa	Greeks aid Cyrus against Artaxerxes
399 B.C.	trial and death of Socrates	
371 B.C.	battle of Leuctra	Thebes defeats Sparta
362 B.C.	battle of Mantinea	Thebes defeats Sparta and Athens
336 B.C.	death of Philip	Alexander becomes king
323 B.C.	death of Alexander	Ptolemy rules Egypt
279 B.C.	Pyrrhus defeats Romans at Asculum	pyrrhic victory
222 B.C.	defeat of Sparta by Achæan League	
220-196 B.C.	first Roman victories in Greece	
146 B.C.	Greece becomes a Roman province	

GREEK HISTORY TIMELINE

DATE	EVENT	DESCRIPTION
c. 1200 B.C.	Trojan War	Trojans defeated by the Greeks
825 B.C.	Lycurgus	reformed laws in Sparta
776 B.C.	first Olympic games	held in Elis
624 B.C.	Draco's code	reformed laws in Athens
c. 594 B.C.	Solon's reforms	further reformed laws in Athens
c. 560 B.C.	coup of Pisistratus	seized the Acropolis in Athens
527 B.C.	death of Pisistratus	
490 B.C.	battle of Marathon	Greeks defeat Persians; Darius I
480 B.C.	battles of Thermopylæ, Salamis	Greeks defeat Persians; Xerxes
479 B.C.	battle of Platæa	final battle against Persians
468 B.C.	Cimon defeats Persians	pursued Persians on land and sea
443-429 B.C.	Pericles dominates Athenian politics	
431-404 B.C.	Peloponnesian War	civil war between Sparta and Athens
430 B.C.	plague at Athens	
401 B.C.	battle of Cunaxa	Greeks aid Cyrus against Artaxerxes
399 B.C.	trial and death of Socrates	
371 B.C.	battle of Leuctra	Thebes defeats Sparta
362 B.C.	battle of Mantinea	Thebes defeats Sparta and Athens
336 B.C.	death of Philip	Alexander becomes king
323 B.C.	death of Alexander	Ptolemy rules Egypt
279 B.C.	Pyrrhus defeats Romans at Asculum	pyrrhic victory
222 B.C.	defeat of Sparta by Achæan League	
220-196 B.C.	first Roman victories in Greece	
146 B.C.	Greece becomes a Roman province	

DRILL QUESTIONS FOR GREEK HISTORY

LESSON 12: Lycurgus

1. He ordered the money of Sparta to be made of iron. _Lycurgus_

2. His reforms made Sparta the greatest military state in Greece. _Lycurgus_

3. Rule by the few. _oligarchy_

4. The slaves of the Spartans. _Helots_

5. The part of Greece that is shaped like a hand. _Peloponnesus_

LESSON 13: Draco and Solon

6. It was said that this Athenian's laws were written in blood. _Draco_

7. The great lawgiver of Athens that made it a government of all the people. _Solon_

8. Rule by the many. _democracy_

9. Rich king of Lydia. _Crœsus_

LESSON 14: Pisistratus the Tyrant

10. Rule by magistrates or councils. _republic_

11. Tyrant of Athens who ordered the poems of Homer to be written down. _Pisistratus_

12. The Acropolis was in this city. _Athens_

13. The sacred tree that grew on the Acropolis. _olive tree_

14. The citadel of Athens. _Acropolis_

15. The only state in Greece that never became a republic. _Sparta_

LESSON 15: Miltiades, the Hero of Marathon

16. King of Persia who initiated the Persian Wars. _Darius_

17. The hero of Marathon. _Miltiades_

18. He ran a marathon to announce the Athenian victory over the Persians. _Phidippides_

LESSON 16: Leonidas at Thermopylæ

19. The hero of Thermopylae. _Leonidas_

20. Elite Spartan military force. _Spartan 300_

21. He ordered his soldiers to scourge the water with 300 lashes. _Xerxes_

22. The narrow channel of water separating Europe from Asia. _Hellespont_

LESSON 17: Themistocles

23. He defeated the Persians at Salamis but later went to their side. _Themistocles_

24. The wooden walls of Athens. _war ships_

LESSON 18: Aristides the Just

25. This rival of Themistocles was banished because he was just. _Aristides_

26. Five famous battles of the Persian Wars. _Marathon, Thermopylae, Salamis, Plataea, Mycale_

27. Last land battle of the Persian Wars. _Plataea_

28. Word that means "to banish" and "earthenware tablet." _ostracism_

29. Persian general during the Persian Wars. _Mardonius_

30. Spartan general who defeated Persians at Plataea. _Pausanias_

31. Last sea battle of the Persian Wars. _Mycale_

LESSON 19: Cimon

32. He began the Long Walls of Athens and defeated the Persians in Asia Minor. _Cimon_

33. The son of Miltiades who hung his bridle in the temple of Athena. _Cimon_

34. The port city of Athens. _Piraeus_

35. Four mile long walls connecting Athens to the sea. _Long Walls_

36. The two legs of Greece. _Athens and Sparta_

37. Two Greek dramatists at the time of Cimon. _Aeschylus and Sophocles_

38. Greek comic playwright. _Aristophanes_

LESSON 20: Pericles

39. Long war that destroyed the Athenian Empire. _Peloponnesian War_

40. He found Athens a city of brick and left it a city of marble. _Pericles_

41. He wrote a history of the Persian Wars and is called the Father of History. _Herodotus_

42. Greek historian who wrote a history of the Peloponnesian War. _Thucydides_

43. The greatest statesman in the history of Greece. _Pericles_

44. He had the Parthenon built while he was leader of Athens. _Pericles_

45. Athens and Thebes were on this part of Greece. _Attica_

46. The name of the Temple of Athena on the Acropolis. _Parthenon_

47. The sculptor who put a likeness of himself on the shield of Athena. _Phidias_

LESSON 21: Alcibiades

48. Naval commander during the Peloponnesian War who was an Athenian fop. __Alcibiades__

49. How the Greeks dated time. __Olympic Games__

50. The Olympic Games were held here. __Elis__

LESSON 22: Lysander

51. Spartan admiral during the Peloponnesian War who captured Athens. __Lysander__

52. He pulled down the Long Walls to the sound of music. __Lysander__

53. Thirty men who were appointed by the Spartans to govern Athens. __Thirty Tyrants__

LESSON 23: Socrates

54. He drank hemlock cheerfully. __Socrates__

55. The love of wisdom. __philosophy__

56. The ugliest person in all of Greece. __Socrates__

57. Greek philosopher who recorded the wisdom of Socrates. __Plato__

58. Socrates' question-and-answer method of teaching. __Socratic Method__

59. Plato's open-air school at Athens. __the Academy__

LESSON 24: Xenophon

60. Three Persian leaders who fought with the Greeks and are found in the Bible.
__Darius, Xerxes, Cyrus__

61. Name of book detailing the March of the 10,000 __Anabasis__

62. Persian king during the March of the 10,000 __Artaxerxes__

63. Student of Socrates who led the 10,000 out of Persia. __Xenophon__

64. Persian general who attempted seizure of his brother's throne. __Cyrus__

LESSON 25: Epaminondas and Pelopidas

65. Two leaders who liberated Thebes from Sparta. __Epaminondas and Pelopidas__

LESSON 26: Philip of Macedonia

66. Father of Alexander who conquered Greece. __Philip of Macedonia__

67. Greek military formation that made the Greeks superior fighters. __phalanx__

LESSON 27: Alexander the Great

68. He could recite the *Iliad* from beginning to end. __Alexander__

69. King of Persia defeated by Alexander. __Darius III__

70. He cried at the age of 30 because he had no new worlds to conquer. _____Alexander_____

71. The name of Alexander's horse. _____Bucephalus_____

72. He cut the Gordian knot. _____Alexander_____

73. Alexander destroyed this city, pulling every building but one to the ground. _____Thebes_____

LESSON 28: Demosthenes

74. He was a stutterer who became the greatest orator of Athens. _____Demosthenes_____

75. Athenian orator who practiced speaking with stones in his mouth. _____Demosthenes_____

76. He copied the famous speeches in Thucydides eight times. _____Demosthenes_____

77. A bitter denunciation of a man or party. _____Philippic_____

78. He urged the Athenians to fight Macedonia the way their forefathers had fought against the Persians.

_____Demosthenes_____

LESSON 29: Aristotle, Zeno, Diogenes, and Apelles

79. He was a cynic who ridiculed the follies of man. _____Diogenes_____

80. Philosophy that counsels man to seek pleasure (peace of mind) in life. _____Epicureanism_____

81. Famous Greek philosopher called the Man of Wisdom. _____Aristotle_____

82. Aristotle's most famous pupil. _____Alexander_____

83. He gave lectures from a porch, from which his philosophy took its name. _____Zeno_____

84. Philosophy that counsels man to endure life without emotion or feeling. _____Stoicism_____

LESSON 30: Ptolemy

85. Great city of learning and trade founded by Alexander. _____Alexandria, Egypt_____

86. This city had the greatest library in the ancient world. _____Alexandria_____

87. Alexander's general whose family became the pharaohs of Egypt. _____Ptolemy_____

88. He encouraged Jews to come to Alexandria and had the Bible translated into Greek.

_____Ptolemy Philadelphus_____

89. The Greek translation of the Bible; translated by 70 scholars in 70 days. _____Septuagint_____

90. Dynasty of Greek rulers in Egypt. _____Ptolemy_____

91. Last of the Ptolemy line. _____Cleopatra_____

92. The country that invented the alphabet and was a great city of commerce. _____Phoenicia_____

93. The canal between the Mediterranean Sea and the Red Sea. _____Suez Canal_____

94. Phoenicia and Carthage practiced this religion. _____Baal worship_____

LESSON 31: Pyrrhus

95. King from Epirus who wanted to be as great as Alexander. _Pyrrhus_

96. Greek mathematician who was killed when Syracuse fell to the Romans. _Archimedes_

97. Victory won with unacceptable losses. _pyrrhic victory_

98. The southern part of Italy was called this. _Magna Graecia_

99. This colony of Tyre became the great rival of Rome. _Carthage_

LESSON 32: Cleomenes III

100. restored the glory of Sparta 600 years after Lycurgus. _Cleomenes III_

101. League of Greek city-states that conquered Sparta. _Achaean League_

LESSON 33: The Fall of Greece

102. The Romans sacked and burned this Greek city. _Corinth_

103. The two countries that conquered Greece after the Peloponnesian War. _Macedonia and Rome_

104. The three Greek cities that tried to rule all of Greece. _Athens, Sparta, Thebes_

105. The world's first and greatest teachers in the natural order. _Greeks_

MAP 1

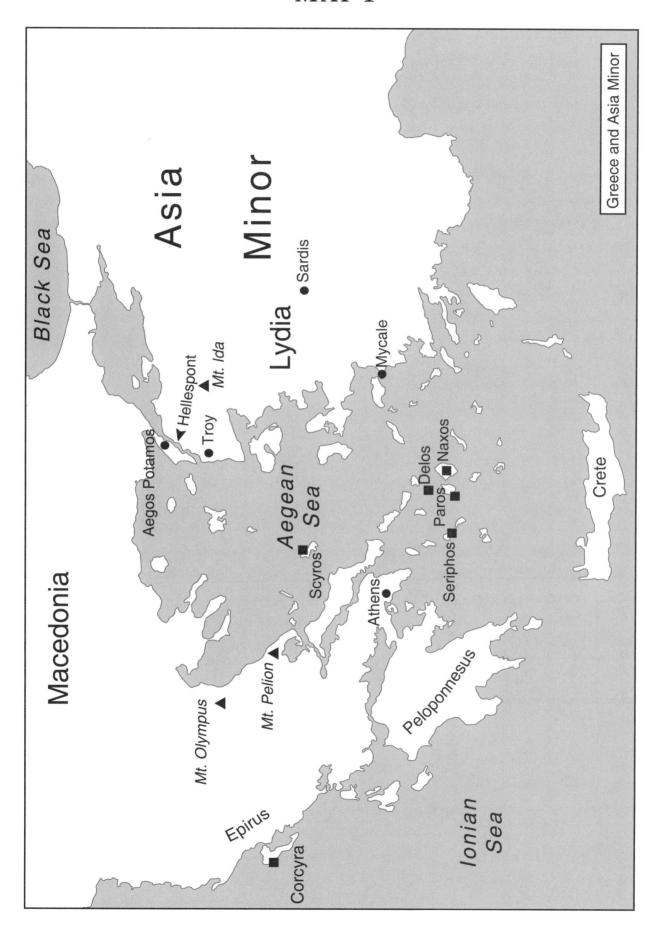

Greece and Asia Minor

Black Sea

Asia

Minor

Macedonia

Lydia

• Sardis

Mycale

Hellespont

Mt. Ida ▲

Troy •

Aegos Potamos •

Aegean
Sea

Delos ■ ■ Naxos

Paros ■

Scyros ■

Seriphos ■

Athens •

Peloponnesus

Crete

Mt. Pelion ▲

Mt. Olympus ▲

Epirus

Corcyra ■

Ionian
Sea

Map 1   125

MAP 2

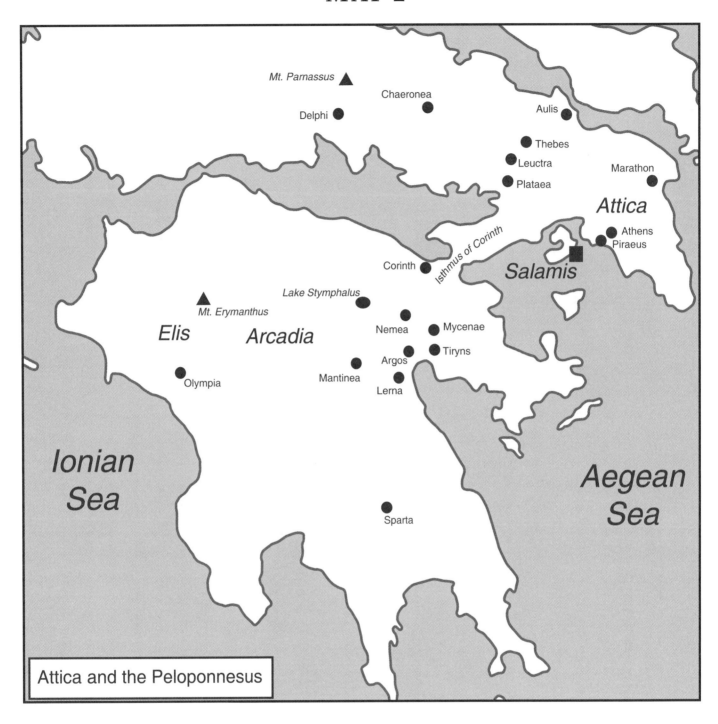

Mt. Parnassus ▲

Chaeronea

Delphi ●

Aulis ●

Thebes ●

Leuctra ●

Marathon ●

Plataea ●

Attica

Isthmus of Corinth

Corinth ●

Salamis ■

Athens ●
Piraeus

Mt. Erymanthus ▲

Lake Stymphalus ●

Elis

Arcadia

Nemea ●

Mycenae ●

Tiryns ●

Argos ●

Olympia ●

Mantinea ●

Lerna ●

*Ionian
Sea*

*Aegean
Sea*

Sparta ●

Attica and the Peloponnesus

MAP 3

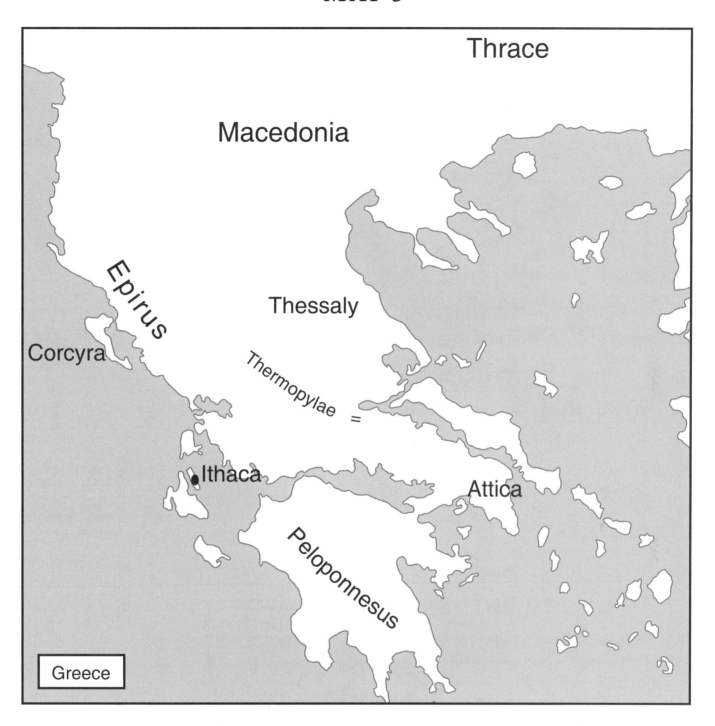

Thrace

Macedonia

Epirus

Corcyra

Thessaly

Thermopylae =

Ithaca

Attica

Peloponnesus

Greece

Map 3   127

MAP 4

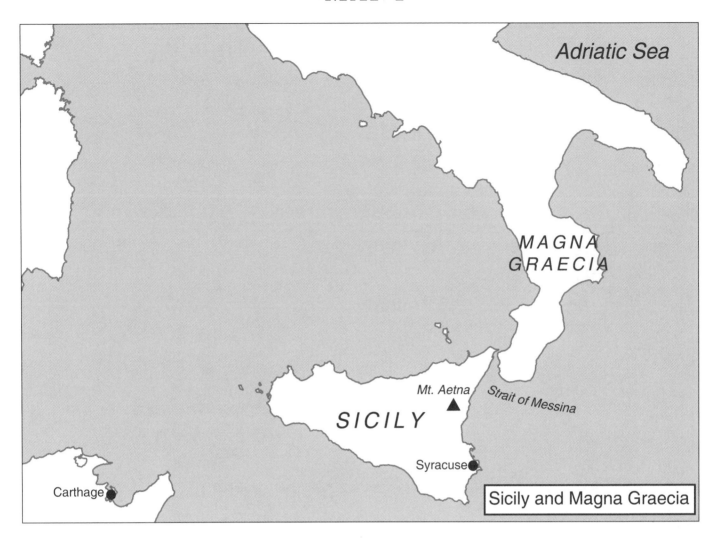

Adriatic Sea

MAGNA GRAECIA

Strait of Messina

Mt. Aetna ▲

SICILY

Syracuse

Carthage

Sicily and Magna Graecia

MAP 5

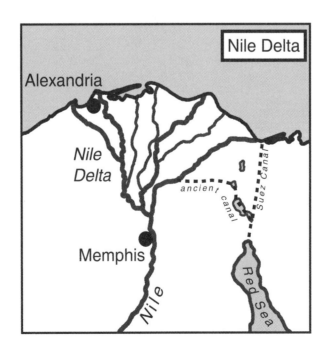

Nile Delta

Alexandria

Nile Delta

ancient canal

Suez Canal

Memphis

Nile

Red Sea

MAP 6

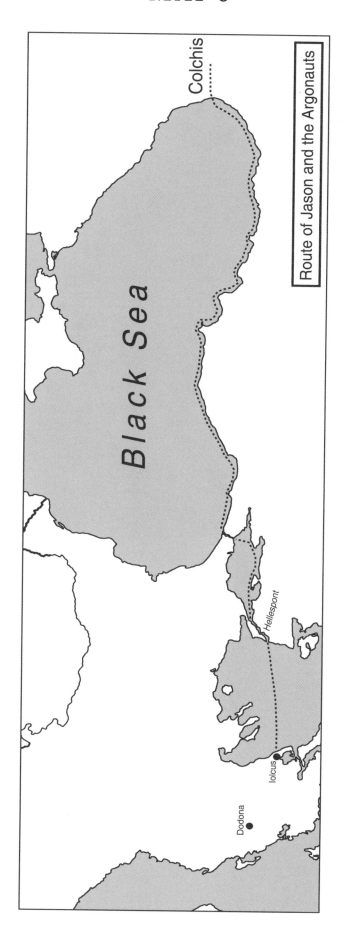

Colchis

Black Sea

Route of Jason and the Argonauts

Hellespont

Iolcus

Dodona

Map 6   129

MAP 7

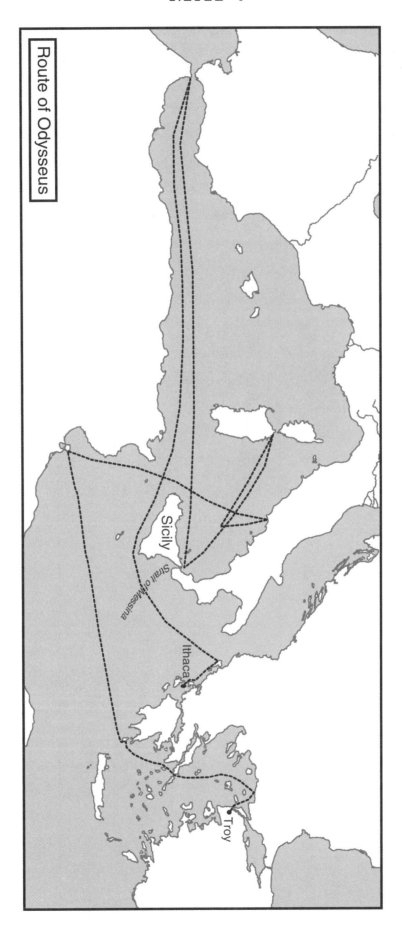

Route of Odysseus

Sicily

Strait of Messina

Ithaca

Troy

MAP 8

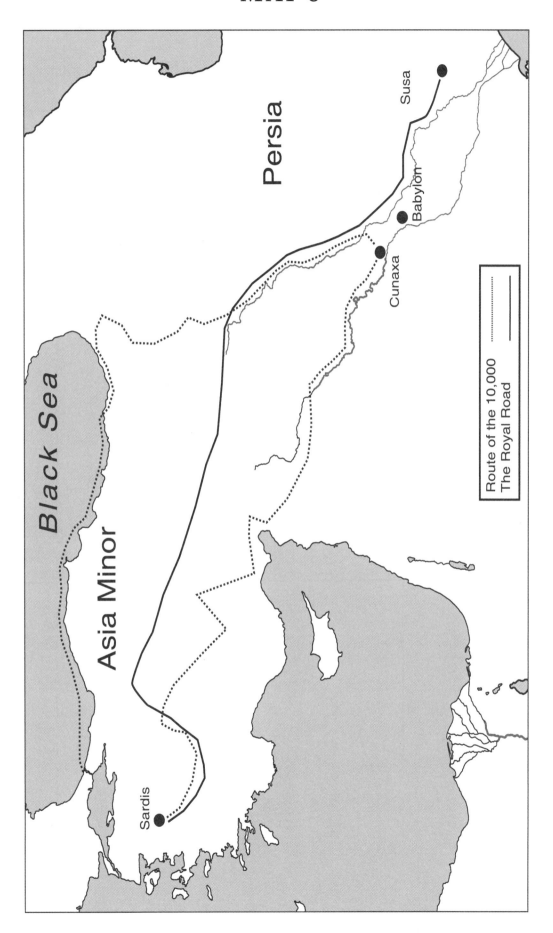

Persia

Susa

Babylon

Cunaxa

Black Sea

Asia Minor

Sardis

Route of the 10,000
The Royal Road

Map 8   131

MAP 9

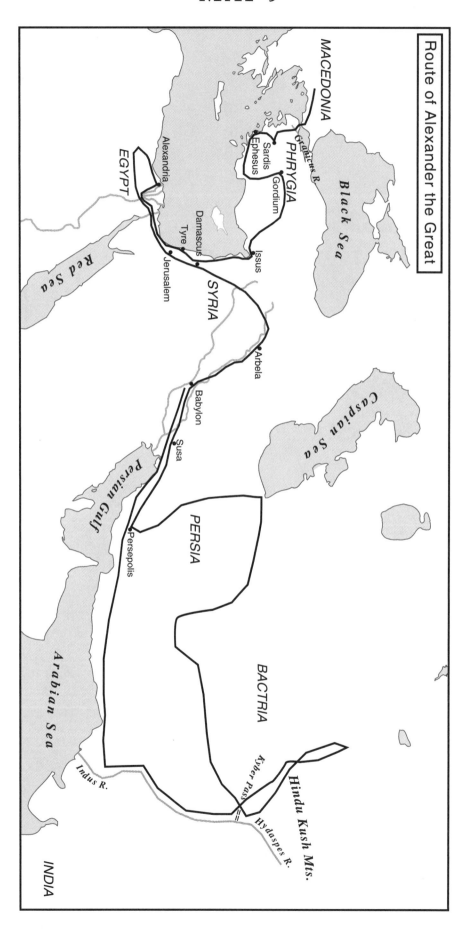

Route of Alexander the Great

MACEDONIA

Granicus R.

Black Sea

EGYPT

Alexandria

Sardis
Ephesus
PHRYGIA
Gordium

Damascus
Tyre
Issus

Jerusalem

SYRIA

Red Sea

Arbela

Babylon

Caspian Sea

Susa

Persian Gulf

Persepolis

PERSIA

BACTRIA

Arabian Sea

Indus R.

Khyber Pass

Hindu Kush Mts.

Hydaspes R.

INDIA

TESTS
(Reproducible)

TEST 1: *Lessons 1-5*

Name:_____ Date:_____ Score:_____

MATCHING: *Choose the answer that best fits the description.*

_____ 1. messenger of the gods

_____ 2. goddess of the underworld

_____ 3. goddess of love

_____ 4. god of fire

_____ 5. god of the oceans

_____ 6. goddess of the moon and hunt

_____ 7. goddess of wisdom

_____ 8. god of love

_____ 9. god of war

_____ 10. goddess of youth

_____ 11. god of the underworld

_____ 12. goddesses of poetry, arts, sciences

_____ 13. king of the Olympian gods

_____ 14. god of the sun

_____ 15. goddess of fire and the hearth

_____ 16. queen of the Olympian gods

_____ 17. first king of the gods

_____ 18. goddess of flowers, grains, and fruit

_____ 19. spun, controlled, and cut the thread of life

_____ 20. giants who aided the first king of the gods

_____ 21. giants who aided his son

_____ 22. river around the underworld

_____ 23. stole fire from the gods

_____ 24. man who survived the flood

_____ 25. watchdog of the underworld

_____ 26. ferryman of the underworld

_____ 27. brought rainbow; bore messages from heaven

_____ 28. made mortals gracious

_____ 29. founder of Thebes

_____ 30. home of the gods

_____ 31. only mortal among the Gorgons

_____ 32. cut off the monster's head

_____ 33. wife of Perseus

_____ 34. tormented the wicked

_____ 35. nymphs with magic treasures

_____ 36. female spirits who help the goddess of grains and fruits

A. Hades	**J.** Cronos	**S.** Hesperides	**AB.** Cyclopes
B. Demeter	**K.** Styx	**T.** the three Graces	**AC.** the Muses
C. Apollo	**L.** Hestia	**U.** Hephaestus	**AD.** Poseidon
D. nymphs	**M.** Athena	**V.** Artemis	**AE.** Hebe
E. Perseus	**N.** Medusa	**W.** Cadmus	**AF.** Hera
F. Eros	**O.** Ares	**X.** Prometheus	**AG.** Deucalion
G. the three Fates	**P.** Persephone	**Y.** Titans	**AH.** Andromeda
H. Hermes	**Q.** Mt. Olympus	**Z.** Aphrodite	**AI.** Zeus
I. Iris	**R.** Charon	**AA.** Cerberus	**AJ.** the three Furies

VOCABULARY: *Choose the answer that best fits the definition.*

_____ 1. food of the gods

_____ 2. source of artistic inspiration

_____ 3. shrine of a prophetic deity

_____ 4. resembling brass

_____ 5. sweet liquid secreted by flowers

_____ 6. group of stars

_____ 7. three-pronged spear

_____ 8. internal layer of mollusk shell

A. trident

B. oracle

C. ambrosia

D. nectar

E. muse

F. mother-of-pearl

G. brazen

H. constellation

COMPREHENSION QUESTIONS: *Answer to the best of your ability. Make sure to use complete sentences and include the names of all important people and places.*

1. How did Zeus become king of the gods?

_____

_____

_____

_____

2. What is the Greek story of the seasons, the fruits, grains, and flowers?

_____

_____

_____

_____

3. How was Greece repopulated after the flood?

_____

_____

_____

_____

4. Recount the story of the founding of Thebes.

_____

_____

_____

_____

5. How was Perseus' fate fulfilled?

_____

_____

_____

_____

GEOGRAPHY: *Identify each location by its letter on the map.*

_____ **1.** Thebes   _____ **3.** Mt. Olympus

_____ **2.** Argos   _____ **4.** Mt. Parnassus

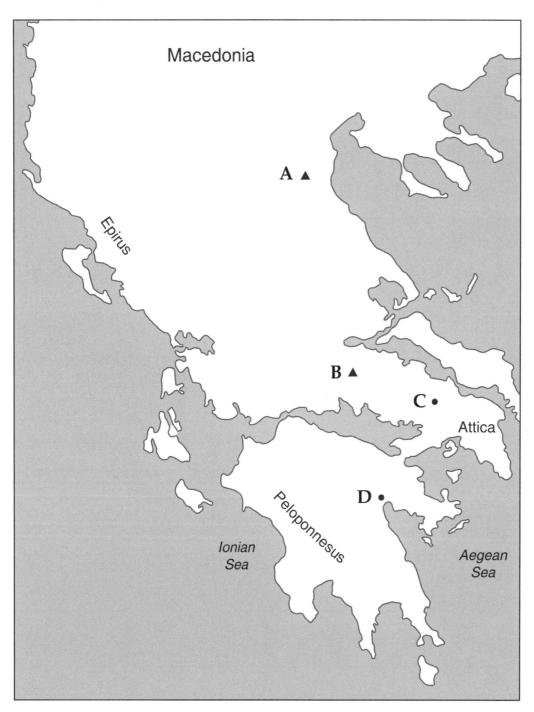

TEST 2: *Lessons 6-10*

Name:_____ Date:_____ Score:_____

MATCHING: *Choose the answer that best fits the description.*

_____ 1. woman whose abduction launched the Trojan War

_____ 2. image of Athena in the temple at Troy

_____ 3. the maze of the Minotaur

_____ 4. hero who went to get the golden fleece

_____ 5. centaur who raised Jason

_____ 6. Jason's ship

_____ 7. twins who sailed with Jason

_____ 8. fell in love with Jason and helped him

_____ 9. held up the sky

_____ 10. king of Troy in the Trojan War

_____ 11. appointed by Zeus to decide which of three goddesses was most beautiful

_____ 12. king of Mycenae and leader of the Greeks in the Trojan War

_____ 13. daughter of Agamemnon who was willing to sacrifice herself for Greece

_____ 14. Agamemnon's soothsayer

_____ 15. king of Sparta in the Trojan War

_____ 16. bravest warrior of the Greeks at Troy

_____ 17. mother of Achilles

_____ 18. friend of Achilles who wore his armor

_____ 19. son of the king of Troy and Trojan champion

_____ 20. mortal son of Zeus who became a god

_____ 21. wife of Hector

_____ 22. founder of Athens

_____ 23. monster of the Labyrinth

_____ 24. hero who killed the monster

_____ 25. king of Crete and keeper of the monster

_____ 26. greatest mythical musician

_____ 27. Greek warrior who found the missing Achilles

_____ 28. beautiful women who lured sailors to their deaths

A. Priam	**H.** Patroclus	**O.** Menelaus	**V.** Labyrinth
B. Thetis	**I.** Paris	**P.** Theseus	**W.** Orpheus
C. Calchas	**J.** Sirens	**Q.** Minotaur	**X.** Atlas
D. Andromache	**K.** Hercules	**R.** Chiron	**Y.** Jason
E. Palladium	**L.** Minos	**S.** Odysseus	**Z.** Medea
F. Argo	**M.** Hector	**T.** Achilles	**AA.** Iphigenia
G. Cecrops	**N.** Helen	**U.** Agamemnon	**AB.** Castor and Pollux

VOCABULARY: *Choose the answer that best fits the definition.*

_____ 1. one who predicts events

_____ 2. adult male deer

_____ 3. belt or sash

_____ 4. mythological creature: half-man, half-horse

_____ 5. front part of a ship

_____ 6. strife; dissension

_____ 7. to break up the earth for farming

_____ 8. sheep's coat of wool

A. girdle

B. discord

C. fleece

D. prow

E. stag

F. centaur

G. soothsayer

H. harrow

WHO SAID THAT?

1. "Beware of the man who wears but one sandal." _____

2. "If my death will help the Greeks, I am ready to die." _____

COMPREHENSION QUESTIONS: *Answer to the best of your ability. Make sure to use complete sentences and include the names of all important people and places.*

1. Describe two of Hercules' labors and how he accomplished them.

_____

_____

_____

_____

2. How was Jason able to take the golden fleece?

_____

_____

_____

_____

3. How did Athens get its name?

_____

_____

_____

_____

_____

_____

4. How did the Trojan War start?

_____

_____

_____

_____

5. What is the story behind the phrase "Achilles' heel"?

_____

_____

_____

GEOGRAPHY: *Identify each location by its letter on the map.*

_____ **1.** Crete   _____ **3.** Athens   _____ **5.** Troy

_____ **2.** Delphi   _____ **4.** Sparta

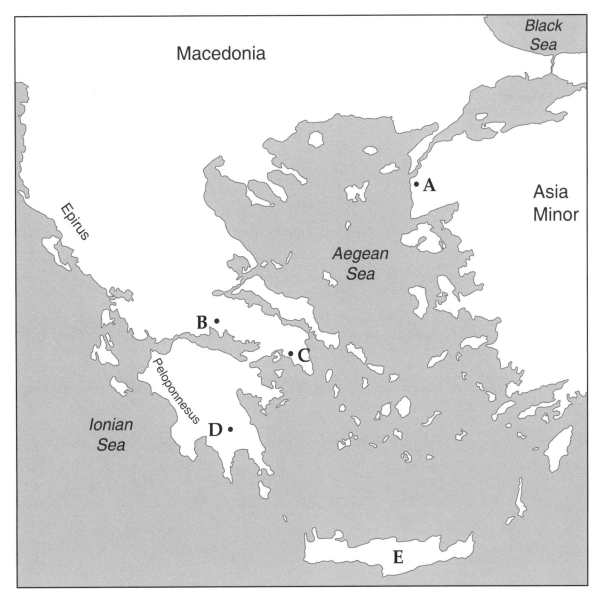

TEST 3: *Lessons 11-15*

Name:_____ Date: _____ Score: _____

MATCHING: *Choose the answer that best fits the description.*

_____ 1. reformers of laws of Athens

_____ 2. reformer of laws of Sparta

_____ 3. epic about the adventures of Odysseus

_____ 4. epic about the Trojan War

_____ 5. king of Persia at the time of the battle of Marathon

_____ 6. proverbial rich king of Lydia

_____ 7. sea-nymph who took care of Odysseus

_____ 8. citadel of Athens

_____ 9. Greek general who won the battle of Marathon

_____ 10. wife of Odysseus

_____ 11. son of Odysseus

_____ 12. home island of Odysseus

_____ 13. approximate date of the Trojan War

_____ 14. became tyrant of Athens by seizing the Acropolis

_____ 15. island princess who found Odysseus on the shore

_____ 16. giant who ate some of Odysseus' men

_____ 17. the two monstrous hazards in the Strait of Messina

_____ 18. god of the winds

_____ 19. sorceress who turned men into animals

_____ 20. conquered people who were made serfs by the Spartans

_____ 21. magistrate of Athens

_____ 22. date of the battle of Marathon

A. Miltiades

B. *Iliad*

C. Circe

D. Draco and Solon

E. Telemachus

F. Pisistratus

G. 490 B.C.

H. c. 1200 B.C.

I. Æolus

J. Calypso

K. Archon

L. Nausicaa

M. *Odyssey*

N. Darius I

O. Cyclops

P. Scylla and Charybdis

Q. Penelope

R. Lycurgus

S. Crœsus

T. Helots

U. Acropolis

V. Ithaca

VOCABULARY: *Choose the answer that best fits the definition.*

_____ 1. government ruled by the few

_____ 2. government ruled by magistrates

_____ 3. sole ruler of a republic city-state

_____ 4. cross-country race of 26.2 miles

_____ 5. to drive off in disorder

_____ 6. frugal and self-disciplined

_____ 7. member of a municipal legislature

_____ 8. throwing spear

_____ 9. a sudden brief violent storm

_____ 10. to recoil involuntarily

_____ 11. weak and soft in attitude or behavior

_____ 12. a city fortress in a commanding position

_____ 13. barely sufficient or adequate

_____ 14. fruit that induces forgetfulness

_____ 15. a lazy person

_____ 16. long adventurous voyage

A.	idler	E.	scanty	I.	oligarchy	M.	effeminate
B.	spartan	F.	tyrant	J.	squall	N.	lotus
C.	citadel	G.	alderman	K.	javelin	O.	odyssey
D.	rout	H.	republic	L.	marathon	P.	flinch

WHO SAID THAT?

1. "Sparta's citizens are her walls." _____

2. "Rejoice! Rejoice! We are victors." _____

3. "I care nothing for gods." _____

4. "Come back with this or upon this." _____

5. "There you will find both earth and water for your master." _____

6. "When I hear whether or not your life has ended nobly, then I shall know whether or not you were really happy." _____

COMPREHENSION QUESTIONS: *Answer to the best of your ability. Make sure to use complete sentences and include the names of all important people and places.*

1. Describe Odysseus' return to his palace.

_____

_____

_____

_____

_____

_____

_____

_____

2. Describe the government and class system of Sparta.

_____

_____

_____

_____

_____

_____

_____

3. What good things did Pisistratus do for Athens?

_____

_____

_____

_____

4. Describe Solon's "shaking off of burdens."

_____

_____

_____

_____

_____

_____

_____

5. How was the news of the victory at Marathon received in Athens, and what happened afterward?

_____

_____

_____

_____

_____

_____

_____

GEOGRAPHY: *Identify each location by its letter on the map.*

_____ **1.** Sparta

_____ **2.** Athens

_____ **3.** Marathon

_____ **4.** Asia Minor

_____ **5.** Sicily

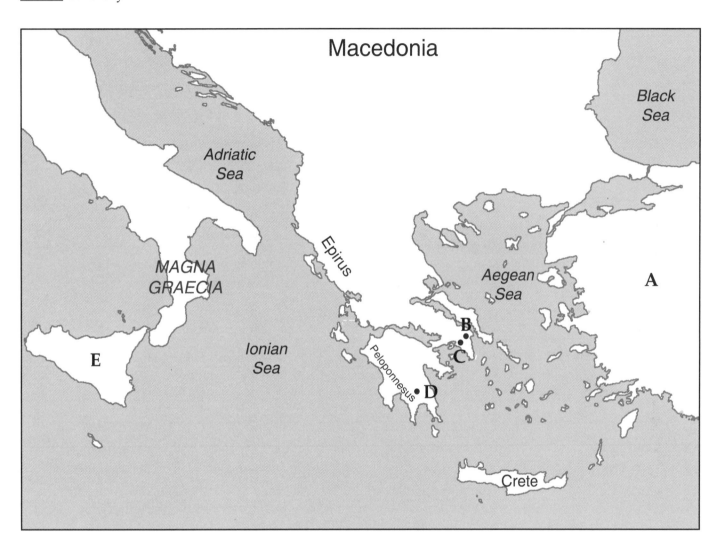

TEST 4: *Lessons 16-20*

Name:_____ Date: _____ Score: _____

MATCHING: *Choose the answer that best fits the description.*

_____ 1. Athenian magistrate and general; called "the Just"

_____ 2. Greek comic playwright of the 5th century B.C.

_____ 3. king of Persia after Darius I, his father

_____ 4. Greek historian of the Persian wars; called "father of history"

_____ 5. son of Miltiades who defeated the Persians

_____ 6. last sea battle between the Greeks and the Persians

_____ 7. last land battle between the Greeks and the Persians

_____ 8. defensive fortifications between Athens and Piræus

_____ 9. two Greek dramatists of the 5th century B.C.

_____ 10. great temple on the Acropolis

_____ 11. Persian general killed at Platæa

_____ 12. date of the battles of Salamis and Thermopylæ

_____ 13. date of the Peloponnesian War

_____ 14. date of the battle of Platæa

_____ 15. Greek sculptor; carved statuary for the Acropolis

_____ 16. Greek general at Platæa

_____ 17. Spartan king who held the pass at Thermopylæ

_____ 18. long war that destroyed the Athenian Empire

_____ 19. wrote a history of the Peloponnesian War

_____ 20. dominant Athenian leader at the start of the Peloponnesian War

A. Xerxes	**F.** 480 B.C.	**K.** Phidias	**P.** 479 B.C.
B. Parthenon	**G.** Cimon	**L.** Aristophanes	**Q.** Mardonius
C. Herodotus	**H.** battle of Mycale	**M.** Leonidas	**R.** Pausanias
D. 431-404 B.C.	**I.** Aristides	**N.** battle of Plataea	**S.** Thucydides
E. Pericles	**J.** Peloponnesian War	**O.** Long Walls	**T.** Aeschylus & Sophocles

VOCABULARY: *Choose the answer that best fits the definition.*

_____ 1. temporary banishment by popular vote

_____ 2. to whip as punishment

_____ 3. to climb with ladders

_____ 4. to destroy; to lay waste; to make unfit for habitation

_____ 5. to disable or disfigure

_____ 6. to expel as punishment

_____ 7. narrow passage of water between two shores

_____ 8. highly infectious, usually fatal epidemic disease

_____ 9. strip of land connecting two larger masses of land

_____ 10. territory ruled by someone

A. banish	**C.** plague	**E.** maim	**G.** scale	**I.** scourge
B. ostracism	**D.** strait	**F.** dominion	**H.** desolate	**J.** isthmus

WHO SAID THAT?

1. "I have never seen him but I am tired of hearing him called 'the Just.'" _____

2. "So much the better, we shall fight in the shade." _____

3. "We fight for all." _____

4. "Athens and Sparta are the two legs of Greece." _____

5. "That of which I am proudest is that no Athenian ever wore mourning because of anything done by me."

_____

COMPREHENSION QUESTIONS: *Answer to the best of your ability. Make sure to use complete sentences and include the names of all important people and places.*

1. What did the army of Xerxes find when it reached Athens, and what did it do?

_____

_____

_____

_____

2. What was the Greek strategy at the battle of Salamis, and what was the outcome?

_____

_____

_____

_____

3. Describe the battle of Platæa, the division of spoils, and the victory offerings.

_____

_____

_____

_____

_____

4. How did Cimon build the Athenian navy, what victories did he win, and what terms did he force on the Persians?

_____

_____

_____

_____

5. What was Pericles' strategy in dealing with the Spartan attack, and what was its effect?

_____

_____

_____

_____

GEOGRAPHY: *Identify each location by its letter on the map.*

_____ **1.** Delphi

_____ **2.** Salamis

_____ **3.** Pass of Thermopylae

_____ **4.** Corinth

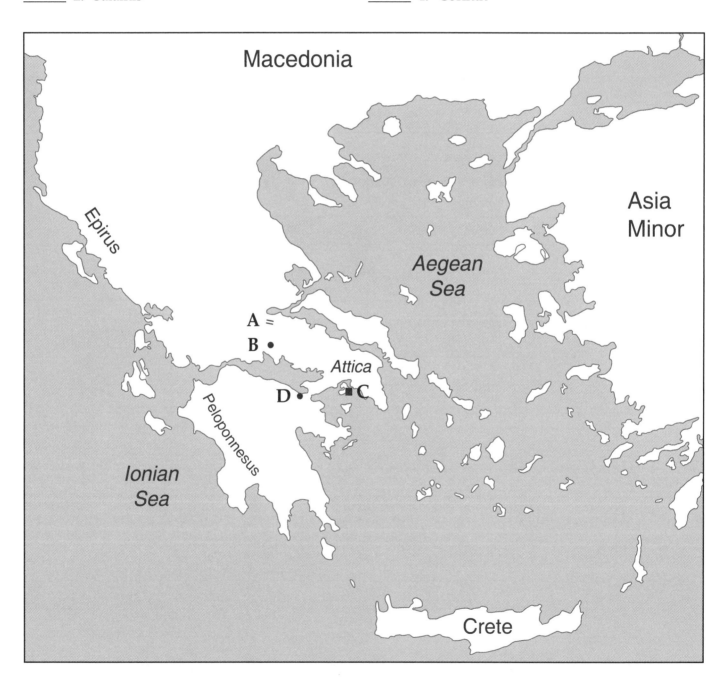

TEST 5: *Lessons 21-25*

Name:_____ Date: _____ Score: _____

MATCHING: *Choose the answer that best fits the description.*

_____ 1. athletic contest used as year-dates by the ancient Greeks

_____ 2. question-and-answer method of teaching

_____ 3. Spartan admiral who captured Athens

_____ 4. Athenian philosopher put to death for disrespecting the gods

_____ 5. Theban general; victor of Mantinea

_____ 6. "The March Upcountry"; history of the retreat of the 10,000

_____ 7. rulers installed at Athens by Sparta

_____ 8. Persian general; attempted to seize his brother's throne

_____ 9. the Persian king from whom the Greeks retreated

_____ 10. hero at the battle of Leuctra with his "sacred band"

_____ 11. founder of the Academy

_____ 12. Athenian commander of the expedition to Sicily

_____ 13. Athenian naval commander who was exiled, then recalled

_____ 14. citadel of Thebes

_____ 15. Greek author of "The March Upcountry"

_____ 16. Athenian who overthrew the tyrants

_____ 17. date of the battle of Mantinea

_____ 18. date of the battle of Cunaxa

_____ 19. date of the battle of Leuctra

_____ 20. date of the first Olympic Games

A. Alcibiades	**F.** 401 B.C.	**K.** Xenophon	**P.** Olympic Games
B. Nicias	**G.** 371 B.C.	**L.** Artaxerxes	**Q.** Thirty Tyrants
C. Lysander	**H.** 362 B.C.	**M.** Epaminondas	**R.** *Anabasis*
D. Thrasybulus	**I.** Socrates	**N.** Pelopidas	**S.** Cadmea
E. 776 B.C.	**J.** Plato	**O.** Cyrus	**T.** Socratic method

VOCABULARY: *Choose the answer that best fits the definition.*

_____ 1. showing artful deception or trickery

_____ 2. fortune; choice

_____ 3. the love and pursuit of wisdom

_____ 4. guard

_____ 5. difficulty; hardship

_____ 6. relative

_____ 7. poisonous plant used for executions in ancient Greece

_____ 8. dandy

_____ 9. four-year period between Olympic Games

_____ 10. a permanent military post

A. hemlock	**C.** garrison	**E.** kinsman	**G.** philosophy	**I.** plight
B. olympiad	**D.** fop	**F.** cunning	**H.** lot	**J.** sentry

WHO SAID THAT?

1. "Thus died the man who was in death the noblest we have ever known, in life, the wisest and the best."

   _____

2. "I see the man." _____

3. "What! Would you have me die guilty?" _____

4. "When the lion's skin is too short, you must patch it with that of a fox." _____

5. "Leuctra and Mantinea are daughters who will keep my name alive." _____

COMPREHENSION QUESTIONS: _Answer to the best of your ability. Make sure to use complete sentences and include the names of all important people and places._

1. Why was the expedition to Sicily undertaken, and what was its outcome?

   _____

   _____

   _____

   _____

   _____

   _____

   _____

2. How was Lysander a fox at Ægos Potamos?

   _____

   _____

   _____

   _____

   _____

   _____

   _____

3. How was Socrates as much an example by his death as by his life?

   _____

   _____

   _____

   _____

   _____

   _____

   _____

4. Why did the Greeks consider the retreat of the 10,000 a victory?

_____

_____

_____

_____

_____

_____

5. How were the tyrants of Thebes overthrown?

_____

_____

_____

_____

_____

_____

_____

_____

_____

_____

GEOGRAPHY: *Identify each location by its letter on the map.*

_____ **1.** Mantinea

_____ **2.** Leuctra

_____ **3.** Aegos Potamos

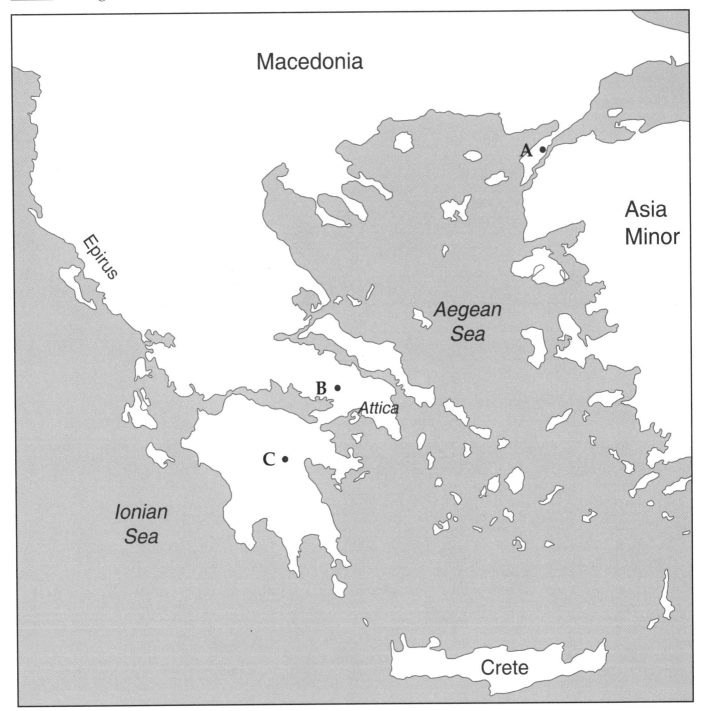

TEST 6: *Lessons 26-30*

Name:_____ Date: _____ Score: _____

MATCHING: *Choose the answer that best fits the description.*

_____ 1. last of the Ptolemies

_____ 2. Alexander's horse

_____ 3. philosopher and teacher of Alexander

_____ 4. founder of the Stoics

_____ 5. orator and author of the Philippics

_____ 6. general who ruled Egypt after Alexander's death

_____ 7. strange philosopher whose followers were called "cynics"

_____ 8. ruler who made Alexandria a center of learning

_____ 9. date of the death of Alexander

_____ 10. date of the death of Philip

_____ 11. painter who painted every day

_____ 12. poet; author of "The Odes"

_____ 13. complicated knot "untied" by Alexander

_____ 14. Alexander's first battle against the Persians

_____ 15. last monarch defeated by Alexander

_____ 16. Alexander's native country

_____ 17. father of Alexander

_____ 18. school of philosophy that teaches simple living

_____ 19. school of philosophy that teaches the pursuit of peace of mind

_____ 20. school of philosophy that assumes men are motivated by selfishness

A. 323 B.C.
B. Apelles
C. Aristotle
D. Bucephalus
E. Cleopatra

F. Cynicism
G. Demosthenes
H. Diogenes
I. Epicureanism
J. Gordian knot

K. battle of Granicus
L. Macedonia
M. Philip II
N. Pindar
O. Porus

P. Ptolemy
Q. Ptolemy Philadelphus
R. Stoicism
S. Zeno
T. 336 B.C.

VOCABULARY: *Choose the answer that best fits the definition.*

_____ 1. compact body of people; military formation

_____ 2. incapable of being morally corrupted

_____ 3. speaking loudly with persuasive effect

_____ 4. a straight line passing from edge to edge through the center of a circle

_____ 5. boundary line of a circle or sphere

_____ 6. Persian provincial governor

_____ 7. a ring with a seal

_____ 8. chariot with blades on the hubs

_____ 9. one who is legally responsible for a minor

_____ 10. soft, spongy center of plant stems

_____ 11. an oppressive power

_____ 12. tool with a long, curved blade

_____ 13. aquatic plant used to make paper

_____ 14. harsh verbal denunciation

_____ 15. feather prepared for use as a writing instrument

A. satrap
B. phalanx
C. pith

D. circumference
E. incorruptible
F. yoke

G. papyrus
H. quill
I. declamation

J. scythe-chariot
K. signet ring
L. diameter

M. philippic
N. scythe
O. guardian

WHO SAID THAT?

1. "Let us be equally energetic and unselfish and just, then we shall triumph." _____

2. "Never a day without a line." _____

3. "To the strongest." _____

4. "I appeal from Philip drunk to Philip sober." _____

5. "My father will leave me nothing to do!" _____

6. "Sell me to someone who wishes a master." _____

COMPREHENSION QUESTIONS: *Answer to the best of your ability. Make sure to use complete sentences and include the names of all important people and places.*

1. What military lessons and lessons in governing did Philip learn from the Spartans?

   _____

   _____

   _____

   _____

   _____

2. List, in order, the key stages of Alexander's conquests.

   a. _____   f. _____

   b. _____   g. _____

   c. _____   h. _____

   d. _____   i. _____

   e. _____   j. _____

3. How did Demosthenes overcome his difficulties as a public speaker?

   _____

   _____

   _____

   _____

   _____

4. Briefly describe the Stoic and Epicurean philosophies in the ancient context.

   _____

   _____

   _____

   _____

   _____

   _____

5. What became of Alexandria, and what became of the Ptolemies?

_____

_____

_____

_____

GEOGRAPHY: *Identify each location by its letter on the map.*

_____ 1. Macedonia

_____ 2. Persia

_____ 3. Egypt

_____ 4. India

_____ 5. Gordium

_____ 6. Alexandria

_____ 7. Babylon

Bonus:

_____ 8. Hydaspes River

_____ 9. Jerusalem

_____ 10. Syria

_____ 11. Arbela

_____ 12. Bactria

_____ 13. Issus

_____ 14. Damascus

_____ 15. Granicus River

_____ 16. Persepolis

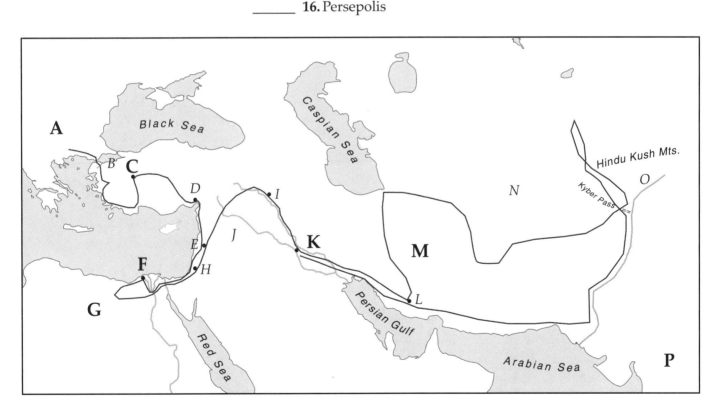

TEST 7: *Lessons 31-33*

Name:_____ Date: _____ Score: _____

MATCHING: *Choose the answer that best fits the description.*

_____	1. mathematician and engineer of Syracuse	**A.** Pyrrhus
_____	2. king of Sparta who tried to restore the laws of Lycurgus	**B.** Agis
_____	3. joint king of Sparta; murdered by Leonidas	**C.** Leonidas
_____	4. king of Epirus who won costly victories against the Romans	**D.** Antigonus
_____	5. league of city-states that defeated Sparta	**E.** 148 B.C.
_____	6. date of the defeat of the Romans by Pyrrhus	**F.** Cleomenes III
_____	7. Macedonian king defeated by Romans	**G.** Archimedes
_____	8. date of the defeat of Sparta by the Achæan League	**H.** 279 B.C.
_____	9. general of the Achæan League	**I.** Aratus
_____	10. date Greece became a Roman province	**J.** Achæan League
_____	11. joint king of Sparta; father of Cleomenes	**K.** Perseus
_____	12. Macedonian king who defeated Sparta	**L.** 222 B.C.

VOCABULARY: *Choose the answer that best fits the definition.*

_____	1. one of the two ruling magistrates of the Roman Republic	**A.** ephor
_____	2. to abandon or renounce	**B.** consul
_____	3. to walk over	**C.** revolt
_____	4. victory with unacceptable losses	**D.** forsake
_____	5. magistrate of Sparta	**E.** tread
_____	6. to rebel; to attempt to overthrow	**F.** pyrrhic victory

TIMELINE: *Match the events to the correct dates.*

_____	1. 1200 B.C.	_____	8. 371 B.C.	**A.** Pyrrhus wins "pyrrhic victory" over Romans
_____	2. 776 B.C.	_____	9. 362 B.C.	**B.** battles of Thermopylæ and Salamis
_____	3. 490 B.C.	_____	10. 336 B.C.	**C.** death of Alexander
_____	4. 480 B.C.	_____	11. 323 B.C.	**D.** Peloponnesian War
_____	5. 479 B.C.	_____	12. 279 B.C.	**E.** Trojan War
_____	6. 431-404 B.C.	_____	13. 222 B.C.	**F.** battle of Marathon
_____	7. 401 B.C.	_____	14. 146 B.C.	**G.** Greece becomes a Roman province
				H. battle of Cunaxa
				I. first Olympic games
				J. battle of Platæa
				K. death of Philip II; Alexander becomes king
				L. battle of Mantinea
				M. battle of Leuctra
				N. defeat of Sparta by Achæan League

WHO SAID THAT?

1. "Another such victory and I shall have to go home alone." _____

2. "If without bloodshed I could have driven from Sparta luxury and extravagance, debts and usury, the riches of the few and the poverty of the many, I should have thought myself the happiest of kings."

_____

COMPREHENSION QUESTIONS: *Answer to the best of your ability. Make sure to use complete sentences and include the names of all important people and places.*

1. Who was Archimedes, and how did he die?

_____

_____

_____

_____

2. What had changed in Sparta, and what did Cleomenes III try to do about it?

_____

_____

_____

_____

_____

_____

3. How did Greek independence end?

_____

_____

_____

_____

_____

_____

4. Who do you believe is the greatest Greek hero and why?

_____

_____

_____

_____

_____

GEOGRAPHY: *Identify each location by its letter on the map.*

_____ **1.** Carthage   _____ **3.** Sicily   _____ **5.** Magna Graecia

_____ **2.** Macedonia   _____ **4.** Syracuse   _____ **6.** Argos

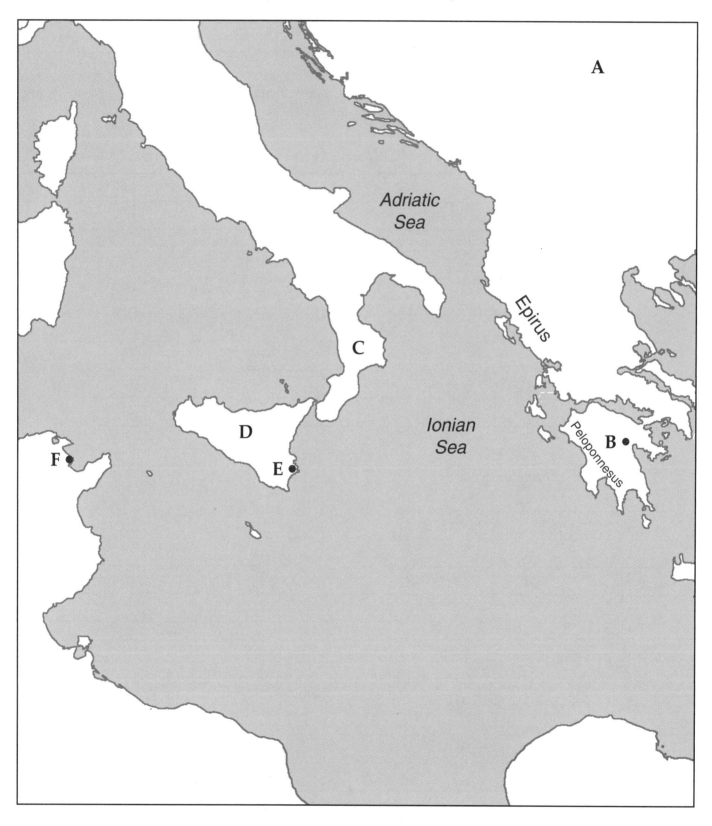

FINAL EXAM

Name:_____ Date: _____ Score: _____

MATCHING: *Choose the answer that best fits the description.*

_____ 1. Aristotle's most famous pupil

_____ 2. It was said that this Athenian's laws were written in blood.

_____ 3. the hero of Marathon

_____ 4. rich king of Lydia

_____ 5. He ran a marathon to announce the Athenian victory over the Persians.

_____ 6. the wooden walls of Athens

_____ 7. Persian general during the Persian Wars

_____ 8. the great lawgiver of Athens that made it a government of all people

_____ 9. the hero of Thermopylae

_____ 10. He ordered his soldiers to scourge the water with 300 lashes.

_____ 11. elite Spartan military force

_____ 12. the port city of Athens

_____ 13. king of Persia who initiated the Persian Wars

_____ 14. four-mile long walls connecting Athens to the sea

_____ 15. He wrote a history of the Persian Wars and is called the Father of History.

_____ 16. tyrant of Athens who ordered the poems of Homer to be written down

_____ 17. He defeated the Persians at Salamis but later went to their side.

_____ 18. Spartan general who defeated Persians at Plataea

_____ 19. Greek comic playwright

_____ 20. This rival of Themistocles was banished because he was just.

_____ 21. the slaves of the Spartans

_____ 22. how the Greeks dated time

_____ 23. Greek philosopher who recorded the wisdom of Socrates

_____ 24. naval commander during the Peloponnesian War, an Athenian fop

_____ 25. Greek historian who wrote a history of the Peloponnesian War

_____ 26. long war that destroyed the Athenian Empire

_____ 27. thirty men who were appointed by the Spartans to govern Athens

_____ 28. Socrates' question-and-answer method of teaching

_____ 29. Persian king during the March of the 10,000

_____ 30. father of Alexander the Great

A. Darius I
B. Xenophon
C. Pausanias
D. Solon
E. Pisistratus
F. Long Walls
G. Aristophanes
H. Darius III
I. Themistocles
J. The Academy
K. Alcibiades
L. Cyrus
M. Phidippides
N. Thucydides
O. Mardonius
P. Artaxerxes
Q. Philip of Macedonia
R. Spartan Three Hundred
S. *Anabasis*
T. Miltiades
U. Plato
V. Thirty Tyrants
W. Herodotus
X. Piraeus
Y. Aristides
Z. Leonidas
AA. Socrates
AB. Olympic Games
AC. Alexander the Great
AD. Peloponnesian War
AE. Helots
AF. Crœsus
AG. Draco
AH. war ships
AI. Xerxes
AJ. Socratic Method
AK. Septuagint

_____ 31. name of the book detailing the March of the 10,000

_____ 32. Plato's open-air school at Athens

_____ 33. king of Persia, defeated by Alexander the Great

_____ 34. Persian general who attempted seizure of his brother's throne

_____ 35. the philosopher who drank hemlock cheerfully and was considered the ugliest man in Greece

_____ 36. student of Socrates who led the 10,000 out of Persia

_____ 37. the name of Alexander's horse

_____ 38. Alexander's general whose family became the pharaohs of Egypt

_____ 39. famous Greek philosopher, called the Man of Wisdom

_____ 40. He was a cynic who ridiculed the follies of man.

_____ 41. the part of Greece that is shaped like a hand

_____ 42. He restored the glory of Sparta 600 years after Lycurgus.

_____ 43. The Romans sacked and burned this Greek city.

_____ 44. the name of the Temple of Athena on the Acropolis

_____ 45. Alexander destroyed this city, pulling almost every building down.

_____ 46. The Acropolis was in this city.

_____ 47. the narrow channel of water separating Europe from Asia

_____ 48. King of Epirus who wanted to be as great as Alexander

_____ 49. the southern part of Italy was called this.

_____ 50. the sculptor who put a likeness of himself on the shield of Athena

_____ 51. Greek translation of the Bible, translated by 70 scholars in 70 days

_____ 52. the citadel of Athens

_____ 53. the country that invented the alphabet and contained a great city of commerce

_____ 54. the sacred tree that grew on the Acropolis

_____ 55. Greek mathematician who was killed when Syracuse fell to the Romans

_____ 56. This colony of Tyre became the great rival of Rome.

_____ 57. He gave lectures from a porch, from which his philosophy took its name.

_____ 58. the canal between the Mediterranean Sea and the Red Sea

_____ 59. Athens and Thebes were in this part of Greece.

_____ 60. last of the Ptolemy line

_____ 61. Phoenicia and Carthage practice this religion.

_____ 62. the world's first and greatest teachers in the natural order

_____ 63. orator who copied Thucydides' speeches eight times and practiced speaking with stones in his mouth

AL. Zeno

AM. Phoenicia

AN. Greeks

AO. Thebes

AP. Attica

AQ. Cleopatra

AR. Suez Canal

AS. olive tree

AT. Archimedes

AU. Acropolis

AV. Carthage

AW. Bucephalus

AX. Corinth

AY. Diogenes

AZ. Ptolemy Philadelphus

BA. Aristotle

BB. Cleomenes III

BC. Magna Graecia

BD. Peloponnesus

BE. Parthenon

BF. Baal worship

BG. Pyrrhus

BH. Athens

BI. Hellespont

BJ. Phidias

BK. Demosthenes

MULTIPLE CHOICE: *Circle the best answer for each question.*

1. What was the last land battle of the Persian Wars?
   a. Mycale
   b. Salamis
   c. Plataea
   d. Marathon

2. What was the last sea battle of the Persian Wars?
   a. Mycale
   b. Salamis
   c. Plataea
   d. Marathon

3. What are the two legs of Ancient Greece?
   a. Macedonia and Athens
   b. Athens and Sparta
   c. Sparta and Corinth
   d. Athens and Thebes

4. Who are the two leaders who liberated Thebes from Sparta?
   a. Epaminondas and Pelopidas
   b. Epaminondas and Philip
   c. Pelopidas and Alexander
   d. Epaminondas and Alexander

5. What are the two countries that conquered Greece after the Peloponnesian War?
   a. Macedonia and Persia
   b. Macedonia and Thrace
   c. Thebes and Rome
   d. Macedonia and Rome

6. Who are the two Greek dramatists at the time of Cimon?
   a. Aristophanes and Euripides
   b. Menander and Euripides
   c. Aristophanes and Sophocles
   d. Aeschylus and Sophocles

7. The philosophy that counsels man to seek pleasure (peace of mind) in life.
   a. Stoicism
   b. Epicureanism
   c. Platonism
   d. Cynicism

8. The philosophy that counsels man to endure life without emotion or feeling.
   a. Epicureanism
   b. Cynicism
   c. Stoicism
   d. Platonism

9. What is the name of the league of Greek city-states that conquered Sparta?
   a. Achaean League
   b. Aegean League
   c. Justice League
   d. Athens League

10. Which is the only Greek city-state that never became a republic?
    a. Thebes
    b. Crete
    c. Athens
    d. Sparta

11. The Olympic Games were held in which city?
    a. Athens
    b. Mt. Olympus
    c. Elis
    d. Sparta

12. Which was a great city of learning and trade, and had the greatest library in the world?
    a. Athens
    b. Alexandria
    c. Rome
    d. Sparta

SHORT ANSWER: *Answer the question to the best of your ability.*

1. List the five famous battles of the Persian Wars.

   _____

2. Name the three Persian leaders who fought with the Greeks and are found in the Bible.

   _____

3. Name the three Greek cities which tried to rule all of Greece.

   _____

4. Name the man who ordered the money of Sparta to be made of iron and reformed the laws of Sparta, making it the greatest military state in Greece.

   _____

5. Name the man, son of Miltiades, who began the Long Walls of Athens, defeated the Persians in Asia Minor, and who hung his bridle in the temple of Athena.

   _____

6. Name the man who was the greatest statesman in the history of Greece, who founded Athens as a city of brick and left it a city of marble. His crowning achievement was building the Parthenon in Athens.

   _____

7. Name the Spartan admiral during the Peloponnesian War who captured Athens and pulled down the Long Walls to the sound of music.

   _____

8. Name the dynasty of Greek rulers in Egypt who encouraged the Jews to come to Alexandria and had the Bible translated into Greek.

   _____

9. Name the man who urged the Athenians to fight Macedonia and became the greatest orator of Athens despite his stutter.

   _____

10. List three famous things Alexander the Great did during his reign.

    _____

    _____

    _____

    _____

    _____

TIMELINE: *Match the events to the correct dates.*

_____ 1. 1200 B.C.

_____ 2. 776 B.C.

_____ 3. 594 B.C.

_____ 4. 490-479 B.C.

_____ 5. 431-404 B.C.

_____ 6. 399 B.C.

_____ 7. 323 B.C.

_____ 8. 146 B.C.

A. Solon reforms the laws of Athens

B. trial and death of Socrates

C. death of Alexander the Great

D. Peloponnesian War

E. Trojan War

F. Greece becomes a Roman province

G. Persian Wars

H. first Olympic Games

VOCABULARY: *Choose the answer that best fits the definition.*

_____ 1. rule by the few

_____ 2. "to banish" and "earthenware tablet"

_____ 3. rule by the many

_____ 4. a bitter denunciation of a man or party

_____ 5. rule by magistrates or councils

_____ 6. the love of wisdom

_____ 7. victory won with unacceptable losses

_____ 8. superior Greek military formation

A. republic

B. Philippic

C. pyrrhic victory

D. oligarchy

E. phalanx

F. ostracism

G. democracy

H. philosophy

BONUS

1. What are the titles of Homer's epic poems describing the Trojan War and Odysseus' return to Ithaca?

   _____

   _____

2. What is the essence of the Stoic philosophy?

   _____

   _____

   _____

TESTS
ANSWER
KEY

TEST 1: *Lessons 1-5* — KEY

Name:_____ Date: _____ Score: _____

MATCHING: *Choose the answer that best fits the description.*

___H___ 1. messenger of the gods

___P___ 2. goddess of the underworld

___Z___ 3. goddess of love

___U___ 4. god of fire

___AD___ 5. god of the oceans

___V___ 6. goddess of the moon and hunt

___M___ 7. goddess of wisdom

___F___ 8. god of love

___O___ 9. god of war

___AE___ 10. goddess of youth

___A___ 11. god of the underworld

___AC___ 12. goddesses of poetry, arts, sciences

___AI___ 13. king of the Olympian gods

___C___ 14. god of the sun

___L___ 15. goddess of fire and the hearth

___AF___ 16. queen of the Olympian gods

___J___ 17. first king of the gods

___B___ 18. goddess of flowers, grains, and fruit

___G___ 19. spun, controlled, and cut the thread of life

___Y___ 20. giants who aided the first king of the gods

___AB___ 21. giants who aided his son

___K___ 22. river around the underworld

___X___ 23. stole fire from the gods

___AG___ 24. man who survived the flood

___AA___ 25. watchdog of the underworld

___R___ 26. ferryman of the underworld

___I___ 27. brought rainbow; bore messages from heaven

___T___ 28. made mortals gracious

___W___ 29. founder of Thebes

___Q___ 30. home of the gods

___N___ 31. only mortal among the Gorgons

___E___ 32. cut off the monster's head

___AH___ 33. wife of Perseus

___AJ___ 34. tormented the wicked

___S___ 35. nymphs with magic treasures

___D___ 36. female spirits who help the goddess of grains and fruits

A. Hades

B. Demeter

C. Apollo

D. nymphs

E. Perseus

F. Eros

G. the three Fates

H. Hermes

I. Iris

J. Cronos

K. Styx

L. Hestia

M. Athena

N. Medusa

O. Ares

P. Persephone

Q. Mt. Olympus

R. Charon

S. Hesperides

T. the three Graces

U. Hephaestus

V. Artemis

W. Cadmus

X. Prometheus

Y. Titans

Z. Aphrodite

AA. Cerberus

AB. Cyclopes

AC. the Muses

AD. Poseidon

AE. Hebe

AF. Hera

AG. Deucalion

AH. Andromeda

AI. Zeus

AJ. the three Furies

VOCABULARY: *Choose the answer that best fits the definition.*

C   **1.** food of the gods

E   **2.** source of artistic inspiration

B   **3.** shrine of a prophetic deity

G   **4.** resembling brass

D   **5.** sweet liquid secreted by flowers

H   **6.** group of stars

A   **7.** three-pronged spear

F   **8.** internal layer of mollusk shell

A. trident

B. oracle

C. ambrosia

D. nectar

E. muse

F. mother-of-pearl

G. brazen

H. constellation

COMPREHENSION QUESTIONS: *Answer to the best of your ability. Make sure to use complete sentences and include the names of all important people and places.*

1. How did Zeus become king of the gods?

   When Zeus grew up, he went to war against Cronos. Zeus was victorious and made Cronos restore to life the children he had swallowed. He divided Cronos' kingdom among them, so they became the gods and goddesses of the world. He made himself king of the gods and his sister Hera queen of the gods.

2. What is the Greek story of the seasons, the fruits, grains, and flowers?

   Hades abducted Persephone and took her to the underworld. Zeus took pity on her and allowed her to return to the earth for a part of each year. When she comes to the earth, it is Spring and Summer. When she leaves, it is Fall and Winter. In the Spring, Demeter causes the fruits, grains, and flowers to grow, with the help of the tree nymphs who make the leaves green, and the water nymphs who water the plants.

3. How was Greece repopulated after the flood?

   Deucalion decided that the oracle's message referred to the earth as the mother and rocks as its bones. As they went down the mountain, Deucalion and Pyrrha cleared their path of stones, which they cast behind them. These turned into bands of young men and women. Deucalion and Pyrrha taught these men and women the useful arts. Together they repopulated the land.

4. Recount the story of the founding of Thebes.

   Armed men sprang from the dragon's teeth sown by Cadmus. A voice commanded Cadmus to throw a stone among the warriors. When he did this, the warriors fought each other until all but five were dead. Cadmus set these to building a city, fulfilling the oracle's instructions and prophecy.

5. How was Perseus' fate fulfilled?

Perseus became good friends with the king of Argos, but accidentally killed him in a
game of quoits. Perseus, now king of Argos but overwhelmed with sorrow, exchanged
his kingdom for the kingdom of Tiryns. After their deaths, he and Andromeda became
stars in the sky.

GEOGRAPHY: *Identify each location by its letter on the map.*

___C___ **1.** Thebes   ___A___ **3.** Mt. Olympus

___D___ **2.** Argos   ___B___ **4.** Mt. Parnassus

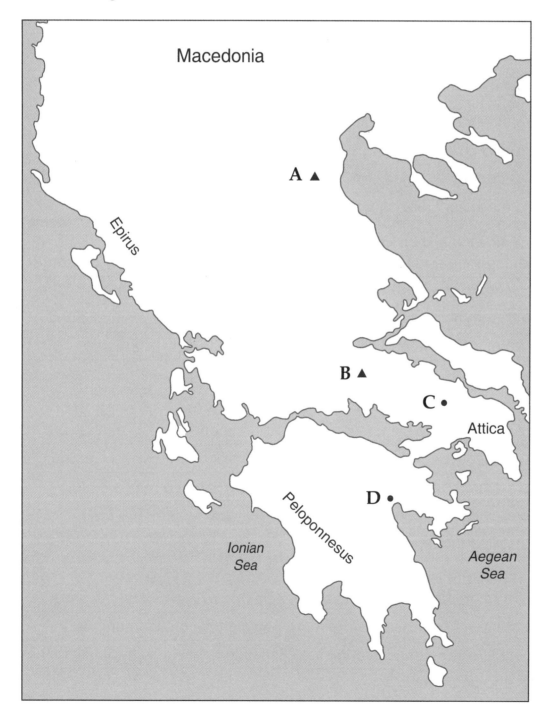

TEST 2: *Lessons 6-10* — KEY

Name:_____ Date:_____ Score:_____

MATCHING: *Choose the answer that best fits the description.*

___N___ **1.** woman whose abduction launched the Trojan War

___E___ **2.** image of Athena in the temple at Troy

___V___ **3.** the maze of the Minotaur

___Y___ **4.** hero who went to get the golden fleece

___R___ **5.** centaur who raised Jason

___F___ **6.** Jason's ship

___AB___ **7.** twins who sailed with Jason

___Z___ **8.** fell in love with Jason and helped him

___X___ **9.** held up the sky

___A___ **10.** king of Troy in the Trojan War

___I___ **11.** appointed by Zeus to decide which of three goddesses was most beautiful

___U___ **12.** king of Mycenae and leader of the Greeks in the Trojan War

___AA___ **13.** daughter of Agamemnon who was willing to sacrifice herself for Greece

___C___ **14.** Agamemnon's soothsayer

___O___ **15.** king of Sparta in the Trojan War

___T___ **16.** bravest warrior of the Greeks at Troy

___B___ **17.** mother of Achilles

___H___ **18.** friend of Achilles who wore his armor

___M___ **19.** son of the king of Troy and Trojan champion

___K___ **20.** mortal son of Zeus who became a god

___D___ **21.** wife of Hector

___G___ **22.** founder of Athens

___Q___ **23.** monster of the Labyrinth

___P___ **24.** hero who killed the monster

___L___ **25.** king of Crete and keeper of the monster

___W___ **26.** greatest mythical musician

___S___ **27.** Greek warrior who found the missing Achilles

___J___ **28.** beautiful women who lured sailors to their deaths

A. Priam
B. Thetis
C. Calchas
D. Andromache
E. Palladium
F. Argo
G. Cecrops

H. Patroclus
I. Paris
J. Sirens
K. Hercules
L. Minos
M. Hector
N. Helen

O. Menelaus
P. Theseus
Q. Minotaur
R. Chiron
S. Odysseus
T. Achilles
U. Agamemnon

V. Labyrinth
W. Orpheus
X. Atlas
Y. Jason
Z. Medea
AA. Iphigenia
AB. Castor and Pollux

VOCABULARY: *Choose the answer that best fits the definition.*

G _____ 1. one who predicts events

E _____ 2. adult male deer

A _____ 3. belt or sash

F _____ 4. mythological creature: half-man, half-horse

D _____ 5. front part of a ship

B _____ 6. strife; dissension

H _____ 7. to break up the earth for farming

C _____ 8. sheep's coat of wool

A. girdle

B. discord

C. fleece

D. prow

E. stag

F. centaur

G. soothsayer

H. harrow

WHO SAID THAT?

1. "Beware of the man who wears but one sandal." _____ oracle of Apollo _____

2. "If my death will help the Greeks, I am ready to die." _____ Iphigenia _____

COMPREHENSION QUESTIONS: *Answer to the best of your ability. Make sure to use complete sentences and include the names of all important people and places.*

1. Describe two of Hercules' labors and how he accomplished them.

   See Lesson 6, Comprehension Question #2.

2. How was Jason able to take the golden fleece?

   Medea, Æetes' daughter, fell in love with Jason and helped him. She gave him ointment as protection against the bulls. She told him to throw a rock into the warriors grown from the dragon's teeth, who proceeded to kill each other. She fed the dragon protecting the fleece a sleeping potion. Thus Jason was able to grab the fleece.

3. How did Athens get its name?

   Athena and Poseidon quarreled over which one would be the chief god of Cecrops' new city. Poseidon's argument was that it would be a great sea power, and Athena's was that it would be a great center of learning. In a contest set by Zeus, Poseidon produced a war horse and Athena produced an olive tree. Zeus decided that olive trees would benefit the city more than war horses, so Athena became the city's goddess and namesake.

4. How did the Trojan War start?

Helen, wife of King Menelaus of Sparta, was known as the most beautiful woman in the world. Paris went to Sparta and stole her away. Menelaus began preparing for war to regain his wife and punish Paris. He had the willing assistance of more than 30 other kings, all rejected suitors of Helen.

5. What is the story behind the phrase "Achilles' heel"?

Achilles' mother, Thetis, could never die. To make her son immortal, she took him to the river Styx, which renders mortals dipped in it invulnerable. She immersed all of his body but the heel, by which she held him. Achilles' heel was his only vulnerable spot.

GEOGRAPHY: *Identify each location by its letter on the map.*

__E__ **1.** Crete   __C__ **3.** Athens   __A__ **5.** Troy

__B__ **2.** Delphi   __D__ **4.** Sparta

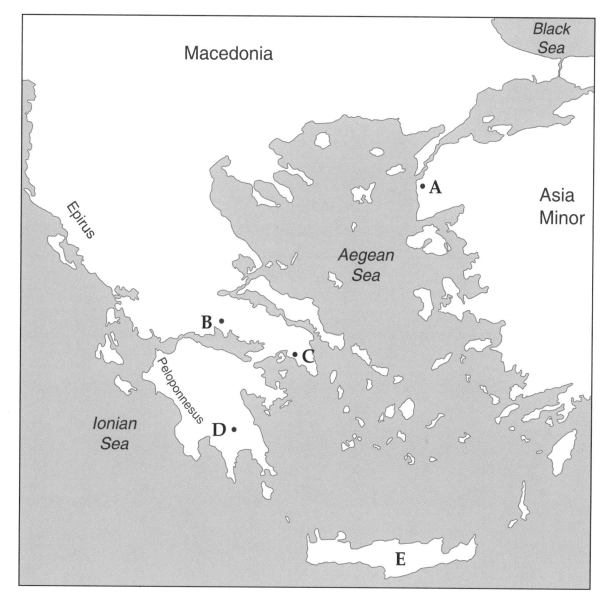

TEST 3: *Lessons 11-15* — KEY

Name:_____ Date:_____ Score:_____

MATCHING: *Choose the answer that best fits the description.*

___D___ 1. reformers of laws of Athens

___R___ 2. reformer of laws of Sparta

___M___ 3. epic about the adventures of Odysseus

___B___ 4. epic about the Trojan War

___N___ 5. king of Persia at the time of the battle of Marathon

___S___ 6. proverbial rich king of Lydia

___J___ 7. sea-nymph who took care of Odysseus

___U___ 8. citadel of Athens

___A___ 9. Greek general who won the battle of Marathon

___Q___ 10. wife of Odysseus

___E___ 11. son of Odysseus

___V___ 12. home island of Odysseus

___H___ 13. approximate date of the Trojan War

___F___ 14. became tyrant of Athens by seizing the Acropolis

___L___ 15. island princess who found Odysseus on the shore

___O___ 16. giant who ate some of Odysseus' men

___P___ 17. the two monstrous hazards in the Strait of Messina

___I___ 18. god of the winds

___C___ 19. sorceress who turned men into animals

___T___ 20. conquered people who were made serfs by the Spartans

___K___ 21. magistrate of Athens

___G___ 22. date of the battle of Marathon

A. Miltiades	**G.** 490 B.C.	**M.** *Odyssey*	**R.** Lycurgus
B. *Iliad*	**H.** c. 1200 B.C.	**N.** Darius I	**S.** Crœsus
C. Circe	**I.** Æolus	**O.** Cyclops	**T.** Helots
D. Draco and Solon	**J.** Calypso	**P.** Scylla and Charybdis	**U.** Acropolis
E. Telemachus	**K.** Archon	**Q.** Penelope	**V.** Ithaca
F. Pisistratus	**L.** Nausicaa		

VOCABULARY: *Choose the answer that best fits the definition.*

_I_ 1. government ruled by the few

_H_ 2. government ruled by magistrates

_F_ 3. sole ruler of a republic city-state

_L_ 4. cross-country race of 26.2 miles

_D_ 5. to drive off in disorder

_B_ 6. frugal and self-disciplined

_G_ 7. member of a municipal legislature

_K_ 8. throwing spear

_J_ 9. a sudden brief violent storm

_P_ 10. to recoil involuntarily

_M_ 11. weak and soft in attitude or behavior

_C_ 12. a city fortress in a commanding position

_E_ 13. barely sufficient or adequate

_N_ 14. fruit that induces forgetfulness

_A_ 15. a lazy person

_O_ 16. long adventurous voyage

A. idler
B. spartan
C. citadel
D. rout

E. scanty
F. tyrant
G. alderman
H. republic

I. oligarchy
J. squall
K. javelin
L. marathon

M. effeminate
N. lotus
O. odyssey
P. flinch

WHO SAID THAT?

1. "Sparta's citizens are her walls." ___Lycurgus___

2. "Rejoice! Rejoice! We are victors." ___Phidippides___

3. "I care nothing for gods." ___Cyclops___

4. "Come back with this or upon this." ___Spartan mothers___

5. "There you will find both earth and water for your master." ___the Spartans___

6. "When I hear whether or not your life has ended nobly, then I shall know whether or not you were really happy." ___Solon___

COMPREHENSION QUESTIONS: *Answer to the best of your ability. Make sure to use complete sentences and include the names of all important people and places.*

1. Describe Odysseus' return to his palace.

   Over 100 suitors from Ithaca and nearby islands had been at the palace and were now pressing Penelope for a decision. Odysseus came to the palace in rags, unrecognized except by his dog. Instructed by Athena, Penelope proposed a contest using Odysseus' bow. Only Odysseus could string and shoot it. He killed all the suitors and resumed his place as king and husband.

2. Describe the government and class system of Sparta.

Sparta was an oligarchy ruled by a few families, traditionally claiming descent from Hercules. There were three classes: the oligarchs who were the only citizens, the Helot serfs consisting of people from cities conquered by Sparta, and a class of people neither serf nor citizen consisting of free farmers, traders, and mechanics, who paid taxes and fought in Sparta's wars.

3. What good things did Pisistratus do for Athens?

He put all the marketplace idlers to work on public projects, he established a large library for everyone, and he commissioned the writing of manuscripts of the epics of Homer.

4. Describe Solon's "shaking off of burdens."

Solon figured that years and even generations of interest were enough. Debts of those who had lost everything were forgiven; houses and farms were returned to their owners; all who had been sold into slavery were freed; debts of those who had not lost everything were reduced by a quarter.

5. How was the news of the victory at Marathon received in Athens, and what happened afterward?

Most Athenians naturally rejoiced at the news. A few traitors, however, signaled the Persian fleet to attack Athens before Miltiades could return. But Miltiades saw the signal and sped back to Athens, preventing a landing and attack by the Persians, who went back to Persia.

GEOGRAPHY: *Identify each location by its letter on the map.*

___D___ **1.** Sparta

___C___ **2.** Athens

___B___ **3.** Marathon

___A___ **4.** Asia Minor

___E___ **5.** Sicily

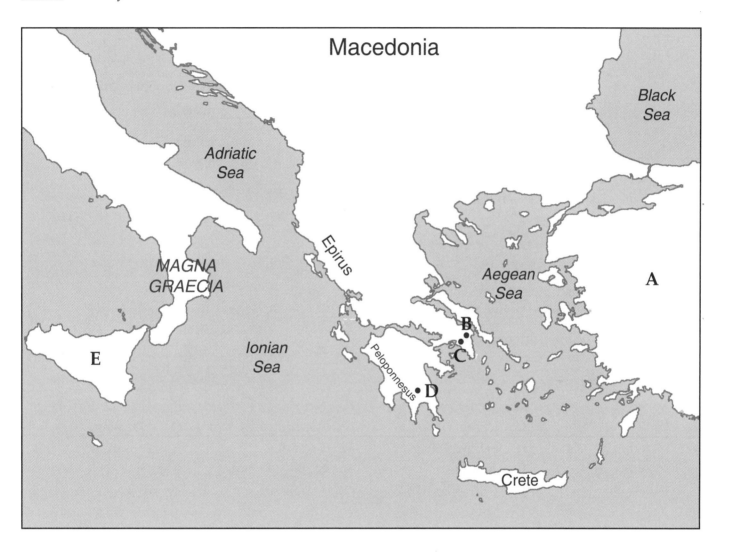

TEST 4: *Lessons 16-20* — KEY

Name:_____ Date: _____ Score: _____

MATCHING: *Choose the answer that best fits the description.*

_____I_____ 1. Athenian magistrate and general; called "the Just"

_____L_____ 2. Greek comic playwright of the 5th century B.C.

_____A_____ 3. king of Persia after Darius I, his father

_____C_____ 4. Greek historian of the Persian wars; called "father of history"

_____G_____ 5. son of Miltiades who defeated the Persians

_____H_____ 6. last sea battle between the Greeks and the Persians

_____N_____ 7. last land battle between the Greeks and the Persians

_____O_____ 8. defensive fortifications between Athens and Piræus

_____T_____ 9. two Greek dramatists of the 5th century B.C.

_____B_____ 10. great temple on the Acropolis

_____Q_____ 11. Persian general killed at Platæa

_____F_____ 12. date of the battles of Salamis and Thermopylæ

_____D_____ 13. date of the Peloponnesian War

_____P_____ 14. date of the battle of Platæa

_____K_____ 15. Greek sculptor; carved statuary for the Acropolis

_____R_____ 16. Greek general at Platæa

_____M_____ 17. Spartan king who held the pass at Thermopylæ

_____J_____ 18. long war that destroyed the Athenian Empire

_____S_____ 19. wrote a history of the Peloponnesian War

_____E_____ 20. dominant Athenian leader at the start of the Peloponnesian War

A. Xerxes	**F.** 480 B.C.	**K.** Phidias	**P.** 479 B.C.
B. Parthenon	**G.** Cimon	**L.** Aristophanes	**Q.** Mardonius
C. Herodotus	**H.** battle of Mycale	**M.** Leonidas	**R.** Pausanias
D. 431-404 B.C.	**I.** Aristides	**N.** battle of Plataea	**S.** Thucydides
E. Pericles	**J.** Peloponnesian War	**O.** Long Walls	**T.** Aeschylus & Sophocles

VOCABULARY: *Choose the answer that best fits the definition.*

_____B_____ 1. temporary banishment by popular vote

_____I_____ 2. to whip as punishment

_____G_____ 3. to climb with ladders

_____H_____ 4. to destroy; to lay waste; to make unfit for habitation

_____E_____ 5. to disable or disfigure

_____A_____ 6. to expel as punishment

_____D_____ 7. narrow passage of water between two shores

_____C_____ 8. highly infectious, usually fatal epidemic disease

_____J_____ 9. strip of land connecting two larger masses of land

_____F_____ 10. territory ruled by someone

A. banish	**C.** plague	**E.** maim	**G.** scale	**I.** scourge
B. ostracism	**D.** strait	**F.** dominion	**H.** desolate	**J.** isthmus

WHO SAID THAT?

1. "I have never seen him but I am tired of hearing him called 'the Just.'" ___Athenian to Aristides___

2. "So much the better, we shall fight in the shade." ___Spartan soldier at Thermopylæ___

3. "We fight for all." ___the Greeks at Salamis___

4. "Athens and Sparta are the two legs of Greece." ___Cimon___

5. "That of which I am proudest is that no Athenian ever wore mourning because of anything done by me."
___Pericles___

COMPREHENSION QUESTIONS: *Answer to the best of your ability. Make sure to use complete sentences and include the names of all important people and places.*

1. What did the army of Xerxes find when it reached Athens, and what did it do?

   Xerxes found Athens almost deserted. His men found an undefended place to cross over the wall. The Athenians who had stayed to defend the city either committed suicide or were killed. The Persians plundered and burned the city.

2. What was the Greek strategy at the battle of Salamis, and what was the outcome?

   The Greeks chose to fight in the strait. This caused confusion and havoc in the large Persian fleet, whose ships were ramming each other or preventing them from fighting effectively. The Greeks destroyed 200 Persian ships with the loss of only 40 of their own.

3. Describe the battle of Platæa, the division of spoils, and the victory offerings.

   After capturing an undefended Athens, Mardonius was met in battle at Platæa by 110,000 Greeks under Pausanias. Aristides was put in field command of the troops. Mardonius was defeated and killed. It took ten days to divide the spoils and bury the dead. A tenth of the spoils was sent to Delphi as an offering to Apollo. Liberty games every fourth year were begun at the battlefield, which was declared sacred.

4. How did Cimon build the Athenian navy, what victories did he win, and what terms did he force on the Persians?

   When the allies of Athens grew tired of warfare, Cimon encouraged them to furnish ships and money. He hired sailors from among the Athenians, drilled them in naval warfare, and took them on several expeditions. He defeated two Persian fleets and a Persian army on land, forcing the Persian king to again agree never to enter the Ægean or come nearer than 50 miles on land.

5. What was Pericles' strategy in dealing with the Spartan attack, and what was its effect?

Pericles' strategy was to concentrate the citizens of the countryside around Athens inside the city itself. Athens was the best fortified city in Greece at the time. But when plague hit the city, the concentration of people inside made the death toll very high and contributed to the eventual defeat of Athens in the war.

GEOGRAPHY: *Identify each location by its letter on the map.*

___B___ **1.** Delphi   ___A___ **3.** Pass of Thermopylae

___C___ **2.** Salamis   ___D___ **4.** Corinth

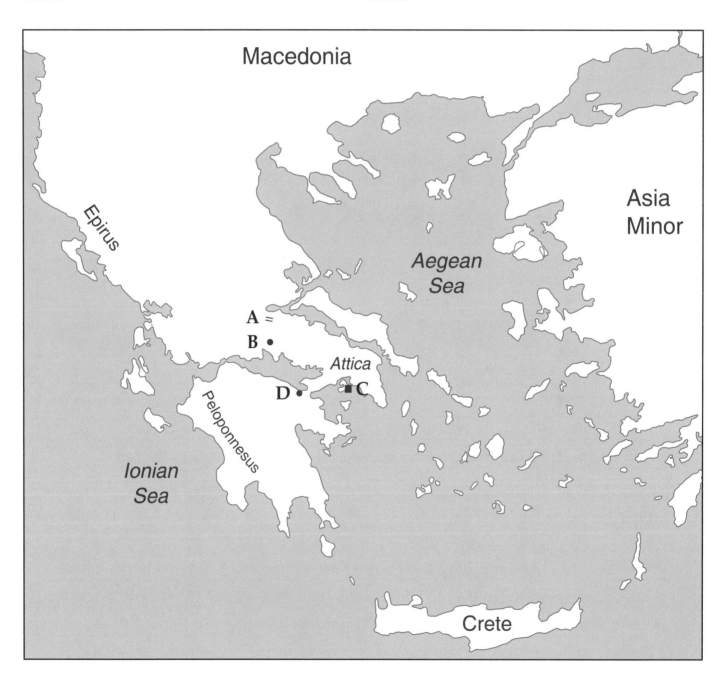

TEST 5: *Lessons 21-25* — KEY

Name:_____ Date: _____ Score: _____

MATCHING: *Choose the answer that best fits the description.*

___P___ 1. athletic contest used as year-dates by the ancient Greeks

___T___ 2. question-and-answer method of teaching

___C___ 3. Spartan admiral who captured Athens

___I___ 4. Athenian philosopher put to death for disrespecting the gods

___M___ 5. Theban general; victor of Mantinea

___R___ 6. "The March Upcountry"; history of the retreat of the 10,000

___Q___ 7. rulers installed at Athens by Sparta

___O___ 8. Persian general; attempted to seize his brother's throne

___L___ 9. the Persian king from whom the Greeks retreated

___N___ 10. hero at the battle of Leuctra with his "sacred band"

___J___ 11. founder of the Academy

___B___ 12. Athenian commander of the expedition to Sicily

___A___ 13. Athenian naval commander who was exiled, then recalled

___S___ 14. citadel of Thebes

___K___ 15. Greek author of "The March Upcountry"

___D___ 16. Athenian who overthrew the tyrants

___H___ 17. date of the battle of Mantinea

___F___ 18. date of the battle of Cunaxa

___G___ 19. date of the battle of Leuctra

___E___ 20. date of the first Olympic Games

A.	Alcibiades	**F.**	401 B.C.	**K.**	Xenophon	**P.**	Olympic Games
B.	Nicias	**G.**	371 B.C.	**L.**	Artaxerxes	**Q.**	Thirty Tyrants
C.	Lysander	**H.**	362 B.C.	**M.**	Epaminondas	**R.**	*Anabasis*
D.	Thrasybulus	**I.**	Socrates	**N.**	Pelopidas	**S.**	Cadmea
E.	776 B.C.	**J.**	Plato	**O.**	Cyrus	**T.**	Socratic method

VOCABULARY: *Choose the answer that best fits the definition.*

___F___ 1. showing artful deception or trickery

___H___ 2. fortune; choice

___G___ 3. the love and pursuit of wisdom

___J___ 4. guard

___I___ 5. difficulty; hardship

___E___ 6. relative

___A___ 7. poisonous plant used for executions in ancient Greece

___D___ 8. dandy

___B___ 9. four-year period between Olympic Games

___C___ 10. a permanent military post

A.	hemlock	**C.**	garrison	**E.**	kinsman	**G.**	philosophy	**I.**	plight
B.	olympiad	**D.**	fop	**F.**	cunning	**H.**	lot	**J.**	sentry

WHO SAID THAT?

1. "Thus died the man who was in death the noblest we have ever known, in life, the wisest and the best."
   Plato

2. "I see the man." Cyrus

3. "What! Would you have me die guilty?" Socrates

4. "When the lion's skin is too short, you must patch it with that of a fox." Lysander

5. "Leuctra and Mantinea are daughters who will keep my name alive." Epaminondas

COMPREHENSION QUESTIONS: *Answer to the best of your ability. Make sure to use complete sentences and include the names of all important people and places.*

1. Why was the expedition to Sicily undertaken, and what was its outcome?
   Alcibiades persuaded the Athenians to send an expedition to Syracuse because it was an ally of Sparta, because Athens needed its resources, and because it was assumed that it would be an easy target. It turned out to be the greatest disaster of the war for Athens, with a total loss of a very large and expensive fleet with all its men.

2. How was Lysander a fox at Ægos Potamos?
   Lysander lined up his ships as if ready to give battle, but when the Athenians approached, he did nothing. He repeated this performance for four days until the Athenians, assuming he was afraid, let their guard down. At this point, Lysander moved in and captured almost the entire Athenian fleet.

3. How was Socrates as much an example by his death as by his life?
   Socrates accepted his sentence gracefully and did not protest his innocence. He did not condemn his accusers or executioner. He used the month grace period he was given to commune with his friends and continue teaching. He taught that death is a passage to a nobler existence. He remained cheerful to the end.

4. Why did the Greeks consider the retreat of the 10,000 a victory?

Confronting the Persians would have been suicide. The retreat, however, was successful and saved the army with few losses. It showed courage and ingenuity in dealing with obstacles and hardship, including terrible weather, lack of food, and unfriendly locals.

5. How were the tyrants of Thebes overthrown?

Pelopidas went in exile to Athens, where he raised a force of other exiles and some Athenians. In the guise of a hunting party, his men made their way to Thebes. The tyrants were gathered at the home of a patriot who was in on the plot, where a few of Pelopidas' men, disguised as women, killed them. Pelopidas went into the houses of two remaining tyrants and killed them. The next morning, the rest of Pelopidas' men came in, and the city rose up with them and retook the Cadmea.

GEOGRAPHY: *Identify each location by its letter on the map.*

___C___ **1.** Mantinea

___B___ **2.** Leuctra

___A___ **3.** Aegos Potamos

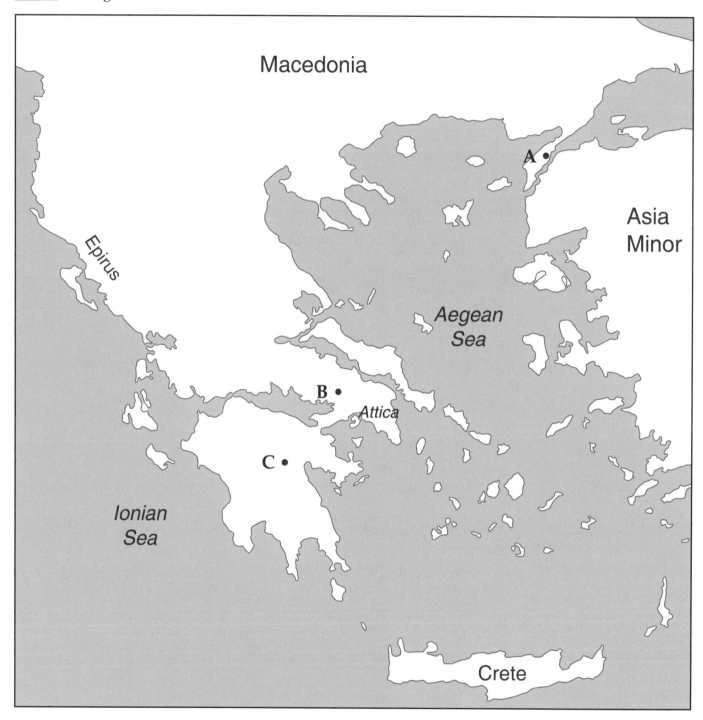

Macedonia

Epirus

Asia Minor

Aegean Sea

A •

B •

Attica

C •

Ionian Sea

Crete

TEST 6: *Lessons 26-30* — KEY

Name:_____ Date: _____ Score: _____

MATCHING: *Choose the answer that best fits the description.*

___E___ **1.** last of the Ptolemies

___D___ **2.** Alexander's horse

___C___ **3.** philosopher and teacher of Alexander

___S___ **4.** founder of the Stoics

___G___ **5.** orator and author of the Philippics

___P___ **6.** general who ruled Egypt after Alexander's death

___H___ **7.** strange philosopher whose followers were called "cynics"

___Q___ **8.** ruler who made Alexandria a center of learning

___A___ **9.** date of the death of Alexander

___T___ **10.** date of the death of Philip

___B___ **11.** painter who painted every day

___N___ **12.** poet; author of "The Odes"

___J___ **13.** complicated knot "untied" by Alexander

___K___ **14.** Alexander's first battle against the Persians

___O___ **15.** last monarch defeated by Alexander

___L___ **16.** Alexander's native country

___M___ **17.** father of Alexander

___R___ **18.** school of philosophy that teaches simple living

___I___ **19.** school of philosophy that teaches the pursuit of peace of mind

___F___ **20.** school of philosophy that assumes men are motivated by selfishness

A.	323 B.C.	**F.**	Cynicism	**K.**	battle of Granicus	**P.** Ptolemy
B.	Apelles	**G.**	Demosthenes	**L.**	Macedonia	**Q.** Ptolemy
C.	Aristotle	**H.**	Diogenes	**M.**	Philip II	Philadelphus
D.	Bucephalus	**I.**	Epicureanism	**N.**	Pindar	**R.** Stoicism
E.	Cleopatra	**J.**	Gordian knot	**O.**	Porus	**S.** Zeno
						T. 336 B.C.

VOCABULARY: *Choose the answer that best fits the definition.*

___B___ **1.** compact body of people; military formation

___E___ **2.** incapable of being morally corrupted

___I___ **3.** speaking loudly with persuasive effect

___L___ **4.** a straight line passing from edge to edge through the center of a circle

___D___ **5.** boundary line of a circle or sphere

___A___ **6.** Persian provincial governor

___K___ **7.** a ring with a seal

___J___ **8.** chariot with blades on the hubs

___O___ **9.** one who is legally responsible for a minor

___C___ **10.** soft, spongy center of plant stems

___F___ **11.** an oppressive power

___N___ **12.** tool with a long, curved blade

___G___ **13.** aquatic plant used to make paper

___M___ **14.** harsh verbal denunciation

___H___ **15.** feather prepared for use as a writing instrument

A.	satrap	**D.**	circumference	**G.**	papyrus	**J.**	scythe-chariot	**M.**	philippic
B.	phalanx	**E.**	incorruptible	**H.**	quill	**K.**	signet ring	**N.**	scythe
C.	pith	**F.**	yoke	**I.**	declamation	**L.**	diameter	**O.**	guardian

WHO SAID THAT?

1. "Let us be equally energetic and unselfish and just, then we shall triumph." ___Demosthenes___

2. "Never a day without a line." ___Apelles___

3. "To the strongest." ___Alexander___

4. "I appeal from Philip drunk to Philip sober." ___Macedonian woman to Philip___

5. "My father will leave me nothing to do!" ___Alexander___

6. "Sell me to someone who wishes a master." ___Diogenes___

COMPREHENSION QUESTIONS: *Answer to the best of your ability. Make sure to use complete sentences and include the names of all important people and places.*

1. What military lessons and lessons in governing did Philip learn from the Spartans?

   Philip knew that Sparta had become a great military power by requiring all of its young men to train as soldiers. He learned from Epaminondas to carefully drill his soldiers and how to arrange them in battle.

   Philip learned not to rule as a tyrant. He acted generously toward conquered states, allowing each to manage their local affairs. General affairs were managed by a council.

2. List, in order, the key stages of Alexander's conquests.

   a. battle of the Granicus   f. Alexandria
   b. Gordium   g. battle of Arbela
   c. battle of Issus   h. Babylon, Susa, and Persepolis
   d. Damascus and the siege of Tyre i. Bactria
   e. Jerusalem and Egypt   j. battle of Hydaspes

3. How did Demosthenes overcome his difficulties as a public speaker?

   To overcome stammering, he practiced speaking with stones in his mouth. To accustom himself to the noise of the public assembly, he practiced speaking at the beach over the roar of the ocean. To correct a habit of lifting one shoulder, he spoke with a sword suspended over the other shoulder. He isolated himself for months practicing. To learn oratory, he studied with the speaker Isæus.

4. Briefly describe the Stoic and Epicurean philosophies in the ancient context.

   The essence of Stoic philosophy is that the world is as it was meant to be and that men should be virtuous and accept whatever comes without complaint. The essence of Epicurean philosophy is that pleasure is the highest good and should be the goal of men. "Pleasure" meant pursuit of knowledge, peace of mind, and avoidance of pain. It was and is often mistakenly taken to mean the pursuit of pleasure through eating, drinking, and living for the day.

5. What became of Alexandria, and what became of the Ptolemies?

Alexandria became a great center of commerce and learning. The library and associated schools became the best in the world, where the best philosophers and scientists came to teach and do research. The Ptolemy line ruled Egypt for over 350 years, into the Roman period. The last monarch of the line was Cleopatra.

GEOGRAPHY: *Identify each location by its letter on the map.*

A   **1.** Macedonia

M   **2.** Persia

G   **3.** Egypt

P   **4.** India

C   **5.** Gordium

F   **6.** Alexandria

K   **7.** Babylon

Bonus:

O   **8.** Hydaspes River

H   **9.** Jerusalem

J   **10.** Syria

I   **11.** Arbela

N   **12.** Bactria

D   **13.** Issus

E   **14.** Damascus

B   **15.** Granicus River

L   **16.** Persepolis

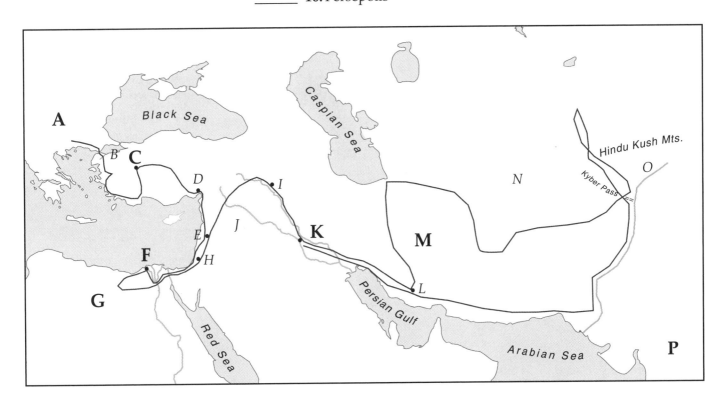

TEST 7: *Lessons 31-33* — KEY

Name:_____ Date:_____ Score:_____

MATCHING: *Choose the answer that best fits the description.*

G	**1.**	mathematician and engineer of Syracuse
F	**2.**	king of Sparta who tried to restore the laws of Lycurgus
B	**3.**	joint king of Sparta; murdered by Leonidas
A	**4.**	king of Epirus who won costly victories against the Romans
J	**5.**	league of city-states that defeated Sparta
H	**6.**	date of the defeat of the Romans by Pyrrhus
K	**7.**	Macedonian king defeated by Romans
L	**8.**	date of the defeat of Sparta by the Achæan League
I	**9.**	general of the Achæan League
E	**10.**	date Greece became a Roman province
C	**11.**	joint king of Sparta; father of Cleomenes
D	**12.**	Macedonian king who defeated Sparta

A. Pyrrhus
B. Agis
C. Leonidas
D. Antigonus
E. 148 B.C.
F. Cleomenes III
G. Archimedes
H. 279 B.C.
I. Aratus
J. Achæan League
K. Perseus
L. 222 B.C.

VOCABULARY: *Choose the answer that best fits the definition.*

B	**1.**	one of the two ruling magistrates of the Roman Republic
D	**2.**	to abandon or renounce
E	**3.**	to walk over
F	**4.**	victory with unacceptable losses
A	**5.**	magistrate of Sparta
C	**6.**	to rebel; to attempt to overthrow

A. ephor
B. consul
C. revolt
D. forsake
E. tread
F. pyrrhic victory

TIMELINE: *Match the events to the correct dates.*

E	**1.** 1200 B.C.	M	**8.** 371 B.C.
I	**2.** 776 B.C.	L	**9.** 362 B.C.
F	**3.** 490 B.C.	K	**10.** 336 B.C.
B	**4.** 480 B.C.	C	**11.** 323 B.C.
J	**5.** 479 B.C.	A	**12.** 279 B.C.
D	**6.** 431-404 B.C.	N	**13.** 222 B.C.
H	**7.** 401 B.C.	G	**14.** 146 B.C.

A. Pyrrhus wins "pyrrhic victory" over Romans
B. battles of Thermopylæ and Salamis
C. death of Alexander
D. Peloponnesian War
E. Trojan War
F. battle of Marathon
G. Greece becomes a Roman province
H. battle of Cunaxa
I. first Olympic games
J. battle of Platæa
K. death of Philip II; Alexander becomes king
L. battle of Mantinea
M. battle of Leuctra
N. defeat of Sparta by Achæan League

WHO SAID THAT?

1. "Another such victory and I shall have to go home alone." ___Pyrrhus___

2. "If without bloodshed I could have driven from Sparta luxury and extravagance, debts and usury, the riches of the few and the poverty of the many, I should have thought myself the happiest of kings."
   Cleomenes III

COMPREHENSION QUESTIONS: *Answer to the best of your ability. Make sure to use complete sentences and include the names of all important people and places.*

1. Who was Archimedes, and how did he die?
   Archimedes was an engineer and mathematician of Greek Syracuse. He invented many devices, including a range of war machines. During the Roman siege of Syracuse, he was killed by a Roman soldier who had no idea who he was.

2. What had changed in Sparta, and what did Cleomenes III try to do about it?
   The citizenry of Sparta had gone from disciplined and well-trained to a lifestyle of luxury and selfishness. Cleomenes committed himself to restoring the laws and disciplines of Lycurgus and Solon. He was opposed by the ephors and many of the citizens. He had the ephors killed, and banished 80 citizens.

3. How did Greek independence end?
   The Greek city-states failed to throw off Macedonian rule, which continued for a century. Macedonia and Epirus were conquered by the Romans, followed by the rest of Greece, which became part of the Roman Empire. This was due in large part to Greek city-states fighting amongst themselves and not showing a united front against their enemies.

4. Who do you believe is the greatest Greek hero and why?
   Answers will vary.

GEOGRAPHY: *Identify each location by its letter on the map.*

___F___ **1.** Carthage   ___D___ **3.** Sicily   ___C___ **5.** Magna Graecia

___A___ **2.** Macedonia   ___E___ **4.** Syracuse   ___B___ **6.** Argos

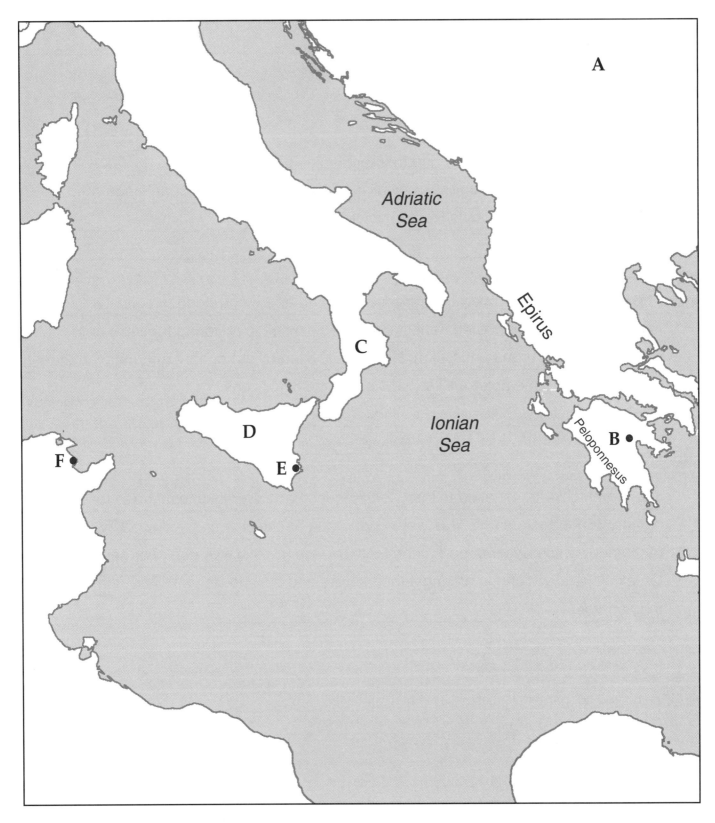

FINAL EXAM — KEY

Name:_____ Date:_____ Score:_____

MATCHING: *Choose the answer that best fits the description.*

__AC__	1.	Aristotle's most famous pupil	**A.** Darius I
__AG__	2.	It was said that this Athenian's laws were written in blood.	**B.** Xenophon
__T__	3.	the hero of Marathon	**C.** Pausanias
__AF__	4.	rich king of Lydia	**D.** Solon
__M__	5.	He ran a marathon to announce the Athenian victory over the Persians.	**E.** Pisistratus
__AH__	6.	the wooden walls of Athens	**F.** Long Walls
__O__	7.	Persian general during the Persian Wars	**G.** Aristophanes
__D__	8.	the great lawgiver of Athens that made it a government of all people	**H.** Darius III
__Z__	9.	the hero of Thermopylae	**I.** Themistocles
__AI__	10.	He ordered his soldiers to scourge the water with 300 lashes.	**J.** The Academy
__R__	11.	elite Spartan military force	**K.** Alcibiades
__X__	12.	the port city of Athens	**L.** Cyrus
__A__	13.	king of Persia who initiated the Persian Wars	**M.** Phidippides
__F__	14.	four-mile long walls connecting Athens to the sea	**N.** Thucydides
__W__	15.	He wrote a history of the Persian Wars and is called the Father of History.	**O.** Mardonius
__E__	16.	tyrant of Athens who ordered the poems of Homer to be written down	**P.** Artaxerxes
__I__	17.	He defeated the Persians at Salamis but later went to their side.	**Q.** Philip of Macedonia
__C__	18.	Spartan general who defeated Persians at Plataea	**R.** Spartan Three Hundred
__G__	19.	Greek comic playwright	**S.** *Anabasis*
__Y__	20.	This rival of Themistocles was banished because he was just.	**T.** Miltiades
__AE__	21.	the slaves of the Spartans	**U.** Plato
__AB__	22.	how the Greeks dated time	**V.** Thirty Tyrants
__U__	23.	Greek philosopher who recorded the wisdom of Socrates	**W.** Herodotus
__K__	24.	naval commander during the Peloponnesian War, an Athenian fop	**X.** Piraeus
__N__	25.	Greek historian who wrote a history of the Peloponnesian War	**Y.** Aristides
__AD__	26.	long war that destroyed the Athenian Empire	**Z.** Leonidas
__V__	27.	thirty men who were appointed by the Spartans to govern Athens	**AA.** Socrates
__AJ__	28.	Socrates' question-and-answer method of teaching	**AB.** Olympic Games
__P__	29.	Persian king during the March of the 10,000	**AC.** Alexander the Great
__Q__	30.	father of Alexander the Great	**AD.** Peloponnesian War
			AE. Helots
			AF. Crœsus
			AG. Draco
			AH. war ships
			AI. Xerxes
			AJ. Socratic Method
			AK. Septuagint

__S__	**31.**	name of the book detailing the March of the 10,000	**AL.** Zeno
__J__	**32.**	Plato's open-air school at Athens	**AM.** Phoenicia
__H__	**33.**	king of Persia, defeated by Alexander the Great	**AN.** Greeks
__L__	**34.**	Persian general who attempted seizure of his brother's throne	**AO.** Thebes
__AA__	**35.**	the philosopher who drank hemlock cheerfully and was considered the ugliest man in Greece	**AP.** Attica
__B__	**36.**	student of Socrates who led the 10,000 out of Persia	**AQ.** Cleopatra
__AW__	**37.**	the name of Alexander's horse	**AR.** Suez Canal
__AZ__	**38.**	Alexander's general whose family became the pharaohs of Egypt	**AS.** olive tree
__BA__	**39.**	famous Greek philosopher, called the Man of Wisdom	**AT.** Archimedes
__AY__	**40.**	He was a cynic who ridiculed the follies of man.	**AU.** Acropolis
__BD__	**41.**	the part of Greece that is shaped like a hand	**AV.** Carthage
__BB__	**42.**	He restored the glory of Sparta 600 years after Lycurgus.	**AW.** Bucephalus
__AX__	**43.**	The Romans sacked and burned this Greek city.	**AX.** Corinth
__BE__	**44.**	the name of the Temple of Athena on the Acropolis	**AY.** Diogenes
__AO__	**45.**	Alexander destroyed this city, pulling almost every building down.	**AZ.** Ptolemy Philadelphus
__BH__	**46.**	The Acropolis was in this city.	**BA.** Aristotle
__BI__	**47.**	the narrow channel of water separating Europe from Asia	**BB.** Cleomenes III
__BG__	**48.**	King of Epirus who wanted to be as great as Alexander	**BC.** Magna Graecia
__BC__	**49.**	the southern part of Italy was called this.	**BD.** Peloponnesus
__BJ__	**50.**	the sculptor who put a likeness of himself on the shield of Athena	**BE.** Parthenon
__AK__	**51.**	Greek translation of the Bible, translated by 70 scholars in 70 days	**BF.** Baal worship
__AU__	**52.**	the citadel of Athens	**BG.** Pyrrhus
__AM__	**53.**	the country that invented the alphabet and contained a great city of commerce	**BH.** Athens
__AS__	**54.**	the sacred tree that grew on the Acropolis	**BI.** Hellespont
__AT__	**55.**	Greek mathematician who was killed when Syracuse fell to the Romans	**BJ.** Phidias
__AV__	**56.**	This colony of Tyre became the great rival of Rome.	**BK.** Demosthenes
__AL__	**57.**	He gave lectures from a porch, from which his philosophy took its name.	
__AR__	**58.**	the canal between the Mediterranean Sea and the Red Sea	
__AP__	**59.**	Athens and Thebes were in this part of Greece.	
__AQ__	**60.**	last of the Ptolemy line	
__BF__	**61.**	Phoenicia and Carthage practice this religion.	
__AN__	**62.**	the world's first and greatest teachers in the natural order	
__BK__	**63.**	orator who copied Thucydides' speeches eight times and practiced speaking with stones in his mouth	

MULTIPLE CHOICE: *Circle the best answer for each question.*

1. What was the last land battle of the Persian Wars?
   a. Mycale
   b. Salamis
   c. Plataea
   d. Marathon

2. What was the last sea battle of the Persian Wars?
   a. Mycale
   b. Salamis
   c. Plataea
   d. Marathon

3. What are the two legs of Ancient Greece?
   a. Macedonia and Athens
   b. Athens and Sparta
   c. Sparta and Corinth
   d. Athens and Thebes

4. Who are the two leaders who liberated Thebes from Sparta?
   a. Epaminondas and Pelopidas
   b. Epaminondas and Philip
   c. Pelopidas and Alexander
   d. Epaminondas and Alexander

5. What are the two countries that conquered Greece after the Peloponnesian War?
   a. Macedonia and Persia
   b. Macedonia and Thrace
   c. Thebes and Rome
   d. Macedonia and Rome

6. Who are the two Greek dramatists at the time of Cimon?
   a. Aristophanes and Euripides
   b. Menander and Euripides
   c. Aristophanes and Sophocles
   d. Aeschylus and Sophocles

7. The philosophy that counsels man to seek pleasure (peace of mind) in life.
   a. Stoicism
   b. Epicureanism
   c. Platonism
   d. Cynicism

8. The philosophy that counsels man to endure life without emotion or feeling.
   a. Epicureanism
   b. Cynicism
   c. Stoicism
   d. Platonism

9. What is the name of the league of Greek city-states that conquered Sparta?
   a. Achaean League
   b. Aegean League
   c. Justice League
   d. Athens League

10. Which is the only Greek city-state that never became a republic?
    a. Thebes
    b. Crete
    c. Athens
    d. Sparta

11. The Olympic Games were held in which city?
    a. Athens
    b. Mt. Olympus
    c. Elis
    d. Sparta

12. Which was a great city of learning and trade, and had the greatest library in the world?
    a. Athens
    b. Alexandria
    c. Rome
    d. Sparta

SHORT ANSWER: *Answer the question to the best of your ability.*

1. List the five famous battles of the Persian Wars.

   Marathon, Thermopylae, Salamis, Plataea, Mycale

2. Name the three Persian leaders who fought with the Greeks and are found in the Bible.

   Darius, Xerxes, Cyrus

3. Name the three Greek cities which tried to rule all of Greece.

   Athens, Sparta, Thebes

4. Name the man who ordered the money of Sparta to be made of iron and reformed the laws of Sparta, making it the greatest military state in Greece.

   Lycurgus

5. Name the man, son of Miltiades, who began the Long Walls of Athens, defeated the Persians in Asia Minor, and who hung his bridle in the temple of Athena.

   Cimon

6. Name the man who was the greatest statesman in the history of Greece, who founded Athens as a city of brick and left it a city of marble. His crowning achievement was building the Parthenon in Athens.

   Pericles

7. Name the Spartan admiral during the Peloponnesian War who captured Athens and pulled down the Long Walls to the sound of music.

   Lysander

8. Name the dynasty of Greek rulers in Egypt who encouraged the Jews to come to Alexandria and had the Bible translated into Greek.

   Ptolemy

9. Name the man who urged the Athenians to fight Macedonia and became the greatest orator of Athens despite his stutter.

   Demosthenes

10. List three famous things Alexander the Great did during his reign.

    Possible answers: He could recite the *Iliad* from beginning to end, he conquered the world by the age of 30, he founded Alexandria (the great city of learning and trade), he cut the Gordian knot, he was taught by Aristotle.

TIMELINE: *Match the events to the correct dates.*

   E   **1.** 1200 B.C.

   H   **2.** 776 B.C.

   A   **3.** 594 B.C.

   G   **4.** 490-479 B.C.

   D   **5.** 431-404 B.C.

   B   **6.** 399 B.C.

   C   **7.** 323 B.C.

   F   **8.** 146 B.C.

A. Solon reforms the laws of Athens

B. trial and death of Socrates

C. death of Alexander the Great

D. Peloponnesian War

E. Trojan War

F. Greece becomes a Roman province

G. Persian Wars

H. first Olympic Games

VOCABULARY: *Choose the answer that best fits the definition.*

   D   **1.** rule by the few

   F   **2.** "to banish" and "earthenware tablet"

   G   **3.** rule by the many

   B   **4.** a bitter denunciation of a man or party

   A   **5.** rule by magistrates or councils

   H   **6.** the love of wisdom

   C   **7.** victory won with unacceptable losses

   E   **8.** superior Greek military formation

A. republic

B. Philippic

C. pyrrhic victory

D. oligarchy

E. phalanx

F. ostracism

G. democracy

H. philosophy

BONUS

1. What are the titles of Homer's epic poems describing the Trojan War and Odysseus' return to Ithaca?

Homer wrote the *Iliad* and *Odyssey*.

2. What is the essence of the Stoic philosophy?

The world is as it was meant to be, and men should be virtuous and accept whatever comes without complaint.